WHAT HAVE YOU DONE FOR ME LATELY?

WHAT HAVE YOU DONE FOR ME LATELY?

Whose yardstick measures your worth?

Jennifer W. Johnson

VMI PUBLISHERS • SISTERS, OREGON

What Have You Done for Me Lately?
© 2008 Jennifer W. Johnson.
All rights reserved.

Published by
VMI Publishers
Sisters, Oregon
www.vmipublishers.com

ISBN: 1-933204-62-1

ISBN 13: 978-1-933204-62-8

Library of Congress Control Number: 2008933070

Printed in the USA

Cover design by Joe Bailen

ACKNOWLEDGMENTS

Thank You, Lord, for providing this wonderful opportunity and for the people that You've placed in my life who supported this initiative completely, patiently and kindly. Thank You for my family who are my inspiration to live in Your light. And for my parents who have given so much in love. Thank You for my publisher who believed in me to carry out Your mission.

TO MY WONDERFUL HUSBAND, A FATHER AND MY BEST FRIEND:
Steve, I love you dearly and forever.

"And I am convinced that nothing can ever separate us from his love.
Death can't, and life can't. The angels can't, and the demons can't.
Our fears for today, our worries about tomorrow, and even
the powers of hell can't keep God's love away.
Whether we are high above the sky or in the deepest ocean, nothing
in all creation will ever be able to separate us
from the love of God that is revealed in
Christ Jesus our Lord"

ROMANS 8:38–39

TABLE OF CONTENTS

INTRODUCTION

What Have You Done for Me Lately?

I t's another day. You've just arrived to the office at the usual time. A cup of coffee is sitting on your desk as you wait for your computer to warm up and display today's e-mails. Your mind is filled with all of the tasks before you. Meetings, conference calls, projections, and a luncheon will occupy the next ten hours of your day.

I'm waiting on you, but that's OK. I can be patient. I am the one who has given you this wonderful opportunity. I want you to be successful and have the very best. The big home, nice car and comfortable lifestyle have all been given to you. A good salary, health insurance, savings plan and a big title are things I've provided for you. I can give you stability and security for anything that you may face in your life. I wonder where you would be if I hadn't provided for you. Let me ask you this question:

"What Have You Done for Me Lately?"

Our response is that the time we give back is invaluable. And more often than not, we give more than what is deserved. A forty-hour week is the maximum we can provide. We have made sacrifices by missing important family obligations to fulfill the responsibilities of the job. We dedicate additional time over the weekend to keep our team on track. Our success is reflected in the revenue we bring to the organization.

Let me ask this question again:

"What Have You Done for Me Lately?"

Perhaps you have confused Me with someone else, or perhaps you don't even know who I am. Are you even aware of all that I have given you? Your talents and gifts were provided to fulfill My purpose. I have not heard from you lately—except occasionally on Sundays, I may hear your voice. By Monday, you have forgotten Me. Your time is given to all of the things that I have given you. The more I give you, the less dependent you become on Me. Have you forgotten Me? Do you even know My name? Let Me ask you this question once more:

"What Have You Done for Me Lately?"

I'm waiting for your answer.

chapter One

WHAT HAS HAPPENED TO OUR CORPORATE WORLD?

*"They see what I do, but they don't really see;
they hear what I say, but they don't understand."*

LUKE 8:10

W hat have you done for me lately?" is a common question (actually a statement) within corporate culture today. "You're only as good as your last sale, title or position in a company" is the corporate world's way of thinking.

These statements are more than phrases. They reflect common sentiments from employees who dedicate endless hours to the business world. As companies continue to expand and compete, each individual's performance becomes even more critical to a company's success. Whether stock prices rise or fall, the pressure continues to increase, and immediate results are expected at every level. Working hard is vital to our means of supporting ourselves in this world. Working smart is critical to our daily success. The question is: How far will we go to achieve success? As leaders in our organization, what sacrifices are we willing to take to grow our business? Will we sacrifice our integrity, or the integrity of others, to protect our own interests? We want to believe that such measures would never take place, but they do every day in the business world, and often, we are the culprits behind the ordeal. The words we use and the actions we take are a reflection of our true character.

This book is designed to help each reader identify his or her true character, uncover hidden motives, and determine where God is in the process. Speaking from experience, there was a time in my life when I placed my personal goals above everything else, making my needs the center of my universe. I accepted positions with companies where my purpose in this world was defined by the title that was given to me.

> *"Always remember that it is the LORD your God who gives you power to become rich, and he does it to fulfill the covenant he made with your ancestors."*

DEUTERONOMY 8:18

My values were measured by the size of my paycheck, and my actions were determined by how I could best be positioned among others in the company. For over twenty years, I've been in sales, management and training. I was never the president or CEO of a company, and I didn't graduate from Harvard. This book is not about how to become a millionaire, or how to grow from rags to riches. It is about helping people who are in a place where I once was. This book is about finding oneself in a world where others have become lost. The examples provided are not meant to inform—but transform—our styles of leadership. It will challenge you to be different, even if it means stepping out of the norm. It's about finding one's purpose beyond the title given to you.

My experience in the business world is typical of many: work hard and succeed by climbing to the top of the corporate ladder. There is nothing wrong with this strategy, and for many, it becomes a way of life. The challenge we face is when our corporate environment becomes our life and center of existence. We measure our life's successes by the size of home we have, the type of car we drive, the titles a company gives us, and the amount of money we have in our bank accounts. People should be rewarded for their hard work, and I do believe working hard instills good values of responsibility, an important part of being able to support ourselves. The problem occurs when we lose balance, spending less time with family, friends, and most importantly, our faith.

As I grew stronger in my faith, my eyes began to open and clearly see what is happening in our corporate culture. I am fortunate to have worked for some of the best companies in the world who taught me to some of life's lessons that can't be found in a college textbook. The examples that I share in this book are reflective of many business cultures today. These examples will help readers open their eyes and gain a better understanding of what's happening today, and most importantly, uncover what changes need to occur to improve the system. Succeeding in today's corporate world will require much more than an education. It will require a system of values that can't be found on a spreadsheet.

Why do I use corporations as my examples, when the contents of this book actually apply to everyday life? A corporate world will demand the majority of one's time. It will place high expectations that will be used to measure one's level of success. Often our work defines our character by the titles given to us. For many, one's work becomes one's life. For others, one's work destroys one's life.

This book is not to discourage anyone from entering the corporate world. It provided me the financial means to help support my family. This book is about opening your eyes and realizing it's not the core of one's existence. It's not the means of survival in this world. Often we become engulfed within the corporate culture and we don't even know it's happening to us. We're spending longer hours in the office. We're placing higher demands on our employees' performance. Our reward becomes the paycheck that's received at the end of the month. Yet, instead of feeling gratified, we feel discouraged.

"If it weren't for the paycheck, I wouldn't be here."
"This job gives me security."
"I doubt there is anything better out there."
"I dread Monday mornings."
"Thank God it's Friday."

Chapter Three

QUALITIES OF
GENUINE LEADERSHIP

"If God has given you leadership ability, take the responsibility seriously.
And if you have a gift for showing kindness to others, do it gladly."

ROMANS 12:8

Paul, an apostle of Jesus Christ, supplied many of the writings for the New Testament, including a letter he wrote to a follower named Titus. Titus was given the responsibility of finding good leaders for the church. Paul's letter highlighted the characteristics of sound leadership.

According to Paul in chapter one of the Book of Titus, a leader should:

1. Not be arrogant or quick-tempered
2. Be hospitable
3. Be encouraging to others
4. Be disciplined
5. Be sensible
6. Not be greedy for money
7. Live a blameless life
8. Not be violent
9. Be fair

10. Stand up for what is right
11. Not be corrupt
12. Have a good conscience
13. Be patient
14. Not speak negatively of others
15. Avoid quarreling

Paul advised Titus to look for leadership qualities that reflected humility and integrity. In business, humility is rarely a quality one speaks of in relation to successful leaders. However, my faith has shown me that what distinguishes genuine leaders from ordinary leaders—even good ones—is one's level of faith. And that is because he or she believes God places people in certain positions for His purpose.

Many of us can become leaders, but few of us will choose to become genuine leaders because our faith does not come before everything else. Therefore, for the purpose of this book, I have defined a "genuine leader" as one who believes God—not the world and its standards—comes first in his or her life. A genuine leader sees a leadership position as a way to fulfill God's purpose over his or her own.

Imagine if our business world applied Paul's criteria and my definition of genuine leadership in the hiring of its leaders and employees? What impact would it have on a company's bottom line? I was a leader in the business world, but never attained genuine leadership, simply because I never considered God's role in my business life. I could see Him in my family life, and He was certainly present in my church life, but when I arrived at the office each morning, I couldn't feel His presence because I never believed business and faith could intertwine. I never considered that God placed me in positions of authority for His purpose. I always believed I was promoted because of my experience and expertise.

Today, leaders may have one or two of the fifteen qualities Paul listed. But, when one looks at their job as an opportunity to serve God first, having a few of these qualities is not enough. Serving God creates a desire to strive for all fifteen.

How do we uncover these types of qualities in people? The first step is reevaluating our hiring criteria and standards for success. The business world has its own criteria for how individuals are measured. Often efficiency and productivity are the only qualities we measure for level of effectiveness.

I have conducted hundreds of interviews in the hiring of candidates, and disappointedly have to admit that I didn't even consider any of the qualities Paul spoke of in my line of questioning. Our questions are based on personal achievements and grade point averages. We look at past performance from a revenue standpoint—not from an integrity standpoint. We love candidates who come from the big ivy schools and the salesperson who claims to make ten new business calls each week. Our standard interview questions may sound like this:

1. How much money do you want to make?
2. Where do you see yourself in five years?
3. What makes you most qualified for this position?

Anyone who has read a textbook on interviewing can come up with the best responses to these questions. If you were interviewing for a job in corporate America, you would respond, "I want to make at least six figures and be in management or running my own company in five years," or "I am most qualified because I am a highly motivated and energetic individual who will stop at nothing to succeed." Chances are you wouldn't get the job unless your response reflected one of these examples.

In fact, many businesses today utilize outside consultants who develop personality profiles and aptitude tests which identify the "ideal" candidate for a specific position. What happens is individuals who score well in areas of integrity, will often lose out to those who score well in areas of assertiveness and aggressiveness.

We admire self-motivation, perseverance, and hard work. Being assertive and outspoken are admirable qualities in the business world. But, are they more important than any of the qualities Paul spoke about? In the sales world, I looked for salespeople who wouldn't take "no" for an answer. Perhaps I need to apologize to every client that my sales team ever worked with. Being a salesperson and not hearing the word "no" only means we are bad listeners.

Paul challenged Titus to look deeper. Perhaps Titus' interview questions would have uncovered more of the qualities from the heart than from previous experience typed on a résumé. Titus was instructed to look for someone with the highest level of integrity. His line of questioning was designed to uncover character qualities. He was to use questions that looked inward instead of outward. We can all be professional interviewees, but only our heart reveals our true character and capabilities.

Genuine leadership is not a criteria, or term we use, when hiring leaders in the corporate world. We say we look for the same qualities in our leaders as Paul expressed, but let's be honest with ourselves. Most companies today don't even have one genuine leader. What most companies have are simply managers.

Managers strive to be genuine leaders, but most never accomplish this role because they don't believe the core values of faith mix with today's business models. The skills of a manager are crucial in keeping the operations of a company running smoothly, but most managers are no more than human computers. They run the daily operations, attend meetings, analyze projections, and furnish necessary reports. They are the individuals who fill an office, but they lack fulfilling a purpose. Their roles are important, but easily replaceable.

Managers are individuals who don't know how to motivate a team and fail to provide valuable insight to help the team become successful. The reason for this is that most managers today are individuals measured solely on efficiency and productivity. A promotion is often based on past job performance.

For example, we assume that if someone is a top salesperson, based on her performance, she would also make a top manager. However, this is rarely the case. Many times our top performers who are placed in leadership roles are not prepared for, or even qualified for a leadership position. When reviewing the qualities provided by Paul, there is no mention of efficiency and past performance. The criteria Paul provides force us to look much deeper than past performance—and right into the heart of an individual instead. Paul is asking Titus to look for genuine leadership qualities that reflect dignity, humility and respect.

It is safe to assume you have a lot of managers. But do you even have one genuine leader?

When companies look closely at their individuals, chances are they can't find any truly genuine leaders. Their qualities can't be found on a résumé.

Genuine leaders are individuals who never allow their integrity to be compromised. In fact, they protect it with their heart, and view integrity as their greatest asset—although it's probably not mentioned on their résumé.

Genuine leaders hold themselves accountable for their actions. They don't look to blame others, but take responsibility for their own mistakes.

They are the ones who never use company money for personal use and always fill out their expense reports with the correct amounts. Their character reflects both strength and humility, and one never hears harsh words from their mouths. Genuine leaders are individuals who seek advice from others, and they have a natural insight about right and wrong—and always do what's right. They lead a life of authenticity.

Genuine leaders are respected and admired for their ability to motivate and serve others, but it's not their title that gives them this ability. They aren't obsessed with their titles or rank, but focus their energy rather on serving and helping their people succeed.

They don't spend countless hours trying to impress others, or use tactics of manipulation to promote themselves within an organization. Genuine leaders are transparent individuals, living their lives as an open book with nothing to hide. That is not to say they are sinless, because we are all born in sin. But overall, genuine leaders are blameless individuals whose lives are admired for their integrity at both work and home.

In over twenty years in the corporate world, I came across only one boss who had qualities of genuine leadership. This gentleman was the CEO of our company, a small business not recognized on the Fortune 500 list. During our start-up years, every dollar was critical to the company's bottom line, and there were times it was questionable whether we would be able to pay our employees. This gentleman never accepted a paycheck until all of his employees were paid. There were many months he went without earning a dime, yet he never complained or applied additional pressure on us to perform better.

He requested advice from all levels of the organization, knowing that there was something he could learn from every person within the company. Titles were nothing but a name on a business card. Everyone played a significant role in the success of the company, and he was deeply grateful for everyone's contributions. If he became aware of any questionable business conduct occurring, he put a stop to it. He had no tolerance for anyone whose behavior was less than dignified.

His goal for the company was to make it as profitable as possible so it could be sold, and those of us who helped build the organization would profit from the sale. Every company has a price, and our CEO was honest and frank about this notion. When investors look at companies for sale, one of the primary things they look at is how to reduce the costs that are currently being incurred. So if the current owner can lower the costs, he has more profitability to show potential buyers.

Sales commissions often make up the largest cost for a company's bottom line. The second largest cost is generally health insurance. Most leaders will cut both in order to gain more value in the eyes of potential investors. However, while they are cutting what is most important to their employees, they neglect to take any cuts themselves. They place their personal interests before the people whose contributions played a role in the company's success.

My CEO was different. He never touched commissions and he never changed our insurance. His philosophy was to sell fairly but not at the risk of hurting the livelihood of those who had grown the company with him. There was no question he would make millions when he sold the company—and rightfully so. Yet, from his perspective, there was a line to be drawn between profitability and greed.

I was one of the managers responsible for building a sales model and hiring a team of salespeople. Our technology was a new concept for advertising and marketing. Therefore, we were not only building a sales model, but also competing against traditional media. Needless to say, it was a difficult job that I felt I was under-qualified to perform.

One evening before heading home, I received a call from our CEO. It was as though he sensed my frustrations and was checking in to see how I was doing. I was too afraid to tell him that I didn't think I was the right person for this opportunity. I certainly didn't want to lose my job. Coincidently, he said it for me. He assured me that no one in the business world had this expertise, but he was confident that I would be one of the individuals to lead this company to success. Instead of criticizing me, he used words of strength and encouragement, giving me what I needed to believe in myself. He exemplified the qualities of genuine leadership Paul wrote about to Titus.

If you have at least one true leader within your organization, consider your company one of the most fortunate in the world. Most individuals leave companies before we recognize their genuine leadership qualities. Genuine leaders are not always the individuals with the big titles and fancy offices. They are not outspoken, but they are often the ones others seek for advice and encouragement. They are truly gratified by their jobs, but their gratification is not centered on those who hired them, or the paycheck that's provided. It comes instead from their faith that they have been placed in this position for a much greater cause.

They are always respectful toward their bosses and never reflect negativity in the office environment. We often overlook the qualities of genuine leaders in our people because our focus is solely based on productivity and contributions to the bottom line. We focus only on what's on paper, and not what lives in one's heart.

Genuine leaders realize there are higher standards than the shallow ones of productivity and the bottom line of the business world that they must live up to—whether they call them God's standards or simply a matter of personal integrity.

One of my closest associates exemplified the qualities of genuine leadership, but not from the corporate world perspective. My associate had been in sales for several years, and was truly an example of genuine leadership for our office, although she didn't have a big title assigned to her.

Management was often critical of her performance, giving her the impression she wasn't driven enough for success. What management failed to see was that her drive for success was not based on making more money, but on wanting to be an example of her faith. It was her compassion and kindness toward her customers and coworkers that made her a true success.

Customers could have purchased from our competition, and most likely would have received satisfactory results. However, customers bought from her because she placed the needs of her customers first. She never compromised business principles to get the sale. In fact, she would turn away business if she truly felt it wasn't in the customer's best interest. Everyone gravitated to her positive attitude. She never spoke harshly of others or participated in the gossip that often transpired around the water cooler.

One of the sales managers at that time had recently been promoted, and yet seemed so lost in her position. Often when we get promoted, we think we know all of the answers, and yet our companies don't even prepare us for what questions to ask. This particular manager was going through a very difficult time. She had lost several of her salespeople, and the unity that once existed within her team was slowly diminishing. On occasions, this manager discussed her situation with my coworker mentioned above, perhaps searching for guidance on how to make things better. To the manager's surprise, my friend gave her a Bible.

How many of us have ever given a Bible to one of our bosses—or even a coworker? When someone asks for advice, aren't we quick to share all of our expertise on the subject matter? In all of my years, I had never encountered this before, nor had I the guts to hand a Bible to one of my bosses. I sadly admit that the Bible was never a source that I would have considered to help me become a better manager. I was simply amazed at the level of conviction behind my friend's faith.

Have you ever worked for a difficult boss whose tactics and words are demeaning? Did you avoid eye contact with him or her or any type of personal interaction at all costs? Most offices today have at least one person who fits this description. Perhaps God wants to soften the hearts of these individuals by using us as an instrument for His purpose. My coworker certainly had this talent within her. I believe her demeanor could soften the heart of any individual on earth because of the strength of her faith.

She viewed these types of situations as an opportunity to reflect her faith, hoping to break through the harsh character traits that often harden our hearts. When we acknowledge God's presence, it becomes challenging to hold any bitterness or resentfulness toward others. We view them as lost sheep, wandering in the dark, and we are the guiding light to help them find their way.

> *"You are the light of the world—like a city on a mountain, glowing in the night for all to see. Don't hide your light under a basket! Instead, put it on a stand and let it shine for all."*
>
> MATTHEW 5:14–15

My coworker had no fear of claiming her faith, and it was her actions that became God's reflection. She never announced out loud to the world that she was a Christian. She didn't have to. Her actions and way of life said it for her.

Companies look for qualities of hardness and arrogance, and not necessarily kindness and compassion. In fact the business world believes the tougher and more aggressive you are, the better leader you will be. I was in management for several years, and feel confident this criterion was the reason for most of my promotions. I appeared to be tough and impenetrable, and anything less would be perceived as weak and incapable. Arrogance gives us a false security of being more knowledgeable, powerful and self-confident; yet it is arrogance that can often be the darkest quality that lives in our hearts. And it eventually leads to destruction.

Jesus saw this dark quality among the religious leaders of His time. They were individuals with important titles who thought they knew the religious laws given to Moses better than anyone else. They considered themselves genuine leaders, but weren't from God's perspective. Having a title does not necessarily make one a genuine leader. When Jesus came into their lives, these leaders became challenged in their way of thinking. Jesus saw through their arrogance and was able to point out their lack of understanding behind the laws given. Arrogance and titles do not always translate into knowledge.

Chapter Four

THE PERSEVERANCE FOR HUMILITY

*"I once thought all these things were so very important, but now
I consider them worthless because of what Christ has done.
Yes, everything else is worthless when compared with the priceless gain of
knowing Christ Jesus my Lord."*

PHILIPPIANS 3:7–8

The apostle Paul was considered a leader among the Jewish people back in his day. He was perceived as an expert in religious law, using his title as a position of authority over the people of Israel. Before his encounter with Christ, Paul had a reputation of persecuting—and even murdering—Christians because by converting to Christianity they were breaking Jewish religious laws. He put his beliefs above those of others. It was his way—or no way—in the matter of people's beliefs.

Leaders today may not go as far as murdering or even persecuting those beneath them, but when our egos create a sense of entitlement, the repercussions can lead to the destruction of an organization.

God had another plan for Paul. A man whose ego was larger than life suddenly became crushed when Jesus appeared to him.

"As he was nearing Damascus on this mission, a brilliant light from heaven suddenly beamed down upon him! He fell to the ground and heard a voice saying to him, 'Saul! Why are you persecuting me?'

ACTS 9:3–4

Can you imagine how Paul (named Saul before he knew Christ) must have felt? His arrogance must have quickly diminished when he encountered one greater than he. This moment in Paul's life transformed him from a leader defined by the world's standards to a genuine leader according to God's standards. This single encounter with Christ changed him forever.

His faith, which now trumped his title, became the foundation behind his influence and authority. His new job in life was to inform as many people about Jesus and how to live their lives like Christ. In essence, he was "hired" by Jesus to educate and promote the Christian faith. God had to bring him down and leave him physically blind for three days. When the Lord restored his vision, He also restored his heart. Paul was able to see the repulsive side of arrogance, as well as the strength behind humility.

How far will we go before we become humbled like Paul? Must we wait for the moment when we have our face-to-face encounter with Christ, who will hold us accountable for our actions? We've been given a lifetime to reach the point of being humbled before God; yet many of us will remain blind to our actions, allowing our pride to justify our sense of entitlement. We strive for self-importance, yet it is a gentle, humble spirit that pleases God most. Humility has a way of revealing our wrongs and creating a desire to make things right in God's eyes.

I've read many business and motivational books throughout my career, and have attended multiple training courses. However, in all of my years, I don't recall "humility" being listed as a quality of an effective leader.

We are told to lead by example, but one of the cardinal rules in the business world is that a leader never admits to being wrong. Let's face it. It's hard to admit when we are wrong. We have trouble admitting this to our children and our spouses, and we carry this over to our work. The perception we have is that admitting we're wrong shows we are weak. Yet, I have learned personally that God can reveal what we consider our greatest weakness to be our greatest strength. Humility, for many, becomes one of the most difficult virtues ever attained.

When we measure ourselves by the world's standards for success—and not God's—humility is never achieved. Instead, we see ourselves through the eyes of others and aim to please those we feel could have a valuable impact on our lives. We are attracted to outward appearances and lifestyles. However, it is the quality of humility found in our hearts that God finds most valuable and pleasing. It is these qualities of humility and kindness where God reveals Himself to others.

Kindness, much like humility, is not a quality that one speaks about in corporate America. However, Jesus showed Paul that kindness was the highest level of intelligence. Even the most arrogant and antagonistic individuals can be kind through the act of humility.

Paul was a leader by the world's standards, but became a genuine leader when he placed God before everything else in his life. We encounter Christ every day, but often these moments are misinterpreted. God reveals Himself in the actions of others, but often it is these actions that are perceived as a weakness instead of strength. When we encounter someone who is kind, we decide they can't lead for fear they may be walked over by others. Yet, it is their kindness that actually becomes one of their greatest strengths.

We miss God's encounters in the corporate world, and often we also miss them at home. As parents, we may become upset when our sons cry once they reach a certain age. The world teaches boys not to cry, and therefore it has become a sign of weakness to be compassionate about things that are important to them. When he was 10, I told my son not to cry over his performance during a baseball game. And yet, I have seen grown men lose the World Series and watched their tears flow as the cameras were rolling. Jesus, the greatest man who ever lived, never hesitated to show tears and compassion for His people.

We also demand perfection from our children, pressing the notion that straight A's are the sole means of measuring one's self-worth. Yet, rarely do we teach (or model for) them compassion and how not to be judgmental toward others. God reveals His patience and kindness in our children. They often work endlessly to overcome their challenges, but we push and push, misinterpreting their less-than-perfect efforts as not trying hard enough.

Humility is more than admitting our mistakes; it also involves acknowledging God's sovereign plan over our lives. When I finally took the time in my life to read the Bible, God was not shy about showing me the ugliness of my pride, providing examples of where I had lived my life aiming to please the world instead of working to please Him. It was one of the most humbling experiences of my life.

It must have been frustrating at times for Jesus, having to explain Himself over and over again to the disciples. They were His children with whom He spent endless hours trying to teach them His ways. Despite the number of times His disciples wandered from His teachings, Jesus never said, "You're not trying hard enough. Now listen this time."

The world has different standards than the standards Christ spoke about with His disciples. We abuse our titles of authority at work and home. Instead of providing guidance and discipline, we belittle those who seem powerless. We confuse discipline with judgment. We believe harshness behind our words is an effective means of achieving positive results, and then wonder why our children yell back at us.

Titles make it easy for arrogance to find its way into our hearts. We see ourselves above everyone else, believing that our position truly makes us more knowledgeable and worthy than those who are beneath us. When our words are used to belittle others, the only discipline we teach is how to drive others away.

After Paul's change of heart, he became harshly criticized and judged by others for his work. So many wanted to bring him down—even to the point of plotting to kill him. The religious leaders who shared his previous way of thinking did everything they could to keep Paul silent. He was strapped in chains and/or confined to a prison cell while writing many of his letters about Christ. However, the more difficult his circumstances, the more powerful Paul's message became.

Paul learned it wasn't his title that gave him authority; it was his faith and humility that was reflected by the way he conducted himself around others. Paul's choice of words appealed to people's hearts and not their egos. He stood for what was right in God's eyes, and anything less was unacceptable. His dedication to his faith became his passion for success. His message wasn't always positive, and his words often pierced the hearts of those who heard or read them. Paul's objective was not to win a popularity contest but to speak truthfully about the actions of others in hopes they would change their hearts also.

There was never a compliant about pain and suffering in his writings—only encouragement, strength and hope. Every situation he encountered was considered a means of becoming stronger in his faith and serving God first in his life. It was not a title, but the humility that stemmed from his faith that exemplified his genuine leadership.

Paul's standards of leadership no longer came from this world, but from God, knowing that His judgment was far more severe than any judgment man could ever subject him to.

Do we have anyone like Paul at our offices? Is there anyone whose actions never waver from faith and doing what is right, regardless of the consequences? Or more personally: Do we hold the same standards at work as we do at home? At home, are the words we use with our families constructive or destructive? That's not to say we should always be positive and flowery with our words.

Many of Paul's writings were direct and forceful. He wasn't one to beat around the bush, but he had no personal agenda as he spoke firmly in his effort to help people follow Christ's ways. His agenda was the same as God's. Paul's words attacked the action, not the person. His words were carefully selected and meant to reflect God's authority—not his own—in his own life and the principles he taught. A humble person thinks before he speaks because he is more concerned about the impact his words will have on others than how his words make him look.

In the corporate world, we like to cut to the chase and tell it like it is. So much of the communication that goes on in e-mails has little or no thought behind the impact it will have on those who read them.

The challenge we face is that the words we select can either build others up or quickly tear them down. When we cut to the chase, the words we use expose how we feel about our position of authority rather than being a constructive way to convey our message.

Leaders like to hear themselves speak, but genuine leaders are humble and prefer seeing the change that occurs in the hearts of those who hear the message. Paul's words spoke to the hearts of his audience. His words were not meant to reflect power or authority, but to serve others in the teachings behind the message of Christ. He stood firmly for what was right and never wavered from reaching toward his objectives. Paul was willing to risk everything to ensure God's message was conveyed to as many individuals as possible who would listen.

"So where does this leave the philosophers, the scholars, and the world's brilliant debaters? God has made them all look foolish and has shown their wisdom to be useless nonsense. Since God in his wisdom saw to it that the world would never find him through human wisdom, he has used our foolish preaching to save all who believe."

1 CORINTHIANS 1:20–21

Imagine if our lives followed the same principles as Paul taught. The challenge we face today is that personal gain has become more important than personal integrity. We are disillusioned if we believe that integrity comes with power, when it is often power that diminishes integrity, since integrity can only come from the heart and not a position of authority. Integrity should be guarded and protected like a child, preventing any ill will from ever touching it.

When titles become our source of significance, we feed on the authority and power they provide. This is often when integrity becomes compromised. Why would we need reason when we have authority?

Genuine leaders place their faith as the most important priority in their lives because it provides the foundation on which their reasoning is built. When we strive for the qualities that Paul presented, the reasoning behind our actions is justified by doing what is right in God's eyes, despite the repercussions we may face from the world. However, in the corporate world, our actions are justified by what we bring to the bottom line.

Why would we need God when we have a team of experts to provide all the answers? This line of reasoning comes from years of experience and the knowledge we've obtained. Having experience is critical, but depending solely on our limited perspective is dangerous. The headlines we read often shape the events of our day. If the market is down, we react negatively, running around like a chicken with its head cut off. When we fall short in meeting our budgets, we act impulsively to uncover every last penny, even if it means not serving our customers or employees well.

Genuine leaders are not reactive to news headlines or missing budgets. They have an acute awareness of the events around them, but what shapes their lives is not the latest news story. Instead, they live by faith and allow its influence to enter into every aspect of their life.

Genuine leaders view success through the eyes of God and not through the eyes of the world. Prayer is an imperative part of their day; they know that without God's hand everything will fall to destruction.

We have come to depend solely on man instead of God in every aspect of our lives. We were born in sin, live in sin, and we turn to the source of sin as our expert, affecting all business and personal matters. As leaders, what we may consider the greatest risk may be God's answer to our problems. The challenge is that we view the risk to be too great. We know what is right but refuse that course of action if the outcome becomes a threat to our bottom line.

However, when we place God first, life takes on a whole different meaning. He becomes our CEO over business and home. Humility takes us from self-serving to a servant role. Genuine leadership strives to serve God's purpose over one's own. That kind of faith affects the way we make decisions and interact with those around us. A parenting role is also a leadership role. As genuine leaders of our homes, we become compassionate toward our children, seeing them for who they are, instead of what they should become.

> *"There is another evil that I have seen as I have watched the world go by. Kings and rulers make a grave mistake if they give foolish people great authority, and if they fail to give people of proven worth their rightful place of dignity. I have even seen servants riding like princes—and princes walking like servants."*

ECCLESIASTES 10:5–7

If you are a leader in your company, perhaps it's time to take a closer look at those who are in management positions and determine whether any of them live with genuine leadership qualities. However, before you begin this process, it is imperative that you first look for these qualities within yourself, and honestly ask yourself, *Where is God in my life?*

"Notice how God is both kind and severe. He is severe to those who disobeyed, but kind to you as you continue to trust in his kindness. But if you stop trusting, you also will be cut off."

ROMANS 11:22

How often do we honestly turn to our faith on matters affecting us both personally and professionally? We say we trust God, but it is our actions—not our words—that reflect the truth. We say God is first in our lives, but only speak of Him occasionally at church. We say we are mature Christians, yet have never studied the Bible. In the corporate world, we keep matters at a distance from our faith. So many of us believe faith and business do not mix, so our actions at work become different than our actions outside the office. A humble spirit shows us how to have the same actions and same beliefs at work and home and church. Nothing changes because of title. In fact, genuine leaders see themselves more accountable for their actions *because* of their titles.

Perhaps it's time to look beyond the words printed on a business card that eventually gets lost or thrown away. Yet, the qualities that live in our heart remain with us forever.

It is a dangerous path to take when we run our departments autonomously without any input from others, or most importantly from God. These types of managers are the empty talkers who are quick to speak and have answers for any possible problem that arises. They know everything and justify their actions simply by virtue of the title they possess. Every company employs at least one of this type of individuals, and as a leader, it is imperative that their motives are uncovered and their personal agendas revealed.

Are they truly experts, or are their motives purely self-gain? There is nothing more rewarding than having someone we consider a mentor or leader seek advice from others. It is even more rewarding when the advice given comes from having a strong foundation of faith and acknowledging God's presence in the outcome.

This may be shocking for many of us to hear, but there are no experts—except God. Many of us want to believe we have all the answers and are very quick to share our viewpoints on every possible subject. God is often the last place we turn to for help—if we turn at all. There is not one problem that God can't handle, and by excluding Him from the matters in our lives, we deny His purpose and existence.

My daughter once made me a bookmark with the phrase that said, "Let God be with you." Being the "expert" that I am, I almost opened my big mouth, wanting to correct the wording to, "May God be with you."

However, after several moments of reading my bookmark over and over again, I realized the best advice that was ever given to me came from a 12-year-old child. I needed to allow God to be with me. That was a humbling moment.

When one aspires for humility, their actions are a reflection of Christ both at work and home because God's advice is always sought. They commit to living an honorable lifestyle, knowing that living by their inner qualities is much more important than outward appearances and titles. We don't necessarily get wiser just because we get older. Age does not necessarily determine wisdom. In fact, many mature adults are less wise simply because they resist changing. They reflect qualities of negativism and resentment.

How quickly we forget all that is good in our lives. Instead we become bitter about the process of aging; yet it is our mortality that removes us from the darkness of this world, into a new place of life. Humble people seek change, knowing that change itself could open the door to endless opportunities.

Besides Paul, another example from the Bible of a humble individual is Moses in the Book of Exodus. It wasn't leading the people out of Egypt that made him a genuine leader. It was his ability to overcome his resistance to change, and most importantly, a humble spirit that acknowledged change itself may be what God provides to fulfill His purpose, and not our own.

We see Moses in Exodus chapter 3 as an older adult, seemingly content with all matters of life. He probably felt there was no need for more knowledge and was content with the simple life of a poor shepherd tending a flock of sheep in Midian. It wasn't until he was probably in his 70s that God began challenging him to be the leader He wanted him to be. God wanted to change the quiet life of Moses because He had heard the cries of the people and His goal was to get them out of Egypt.

Moses resisted at first (Exodus 4), but eventually he accepted the change. Most importantly, humility showed him that his life was not his own. Just as God places us in positions of authority, He placed Moses in a position to fulfill God's purpose. The question we face today, both personally and professionally is: Whose purpose do we want to fulfill?

Many of us will never gain the humility, wisdom and leadership ability that Moses did simply because we never place God's purpose first in our lives. However, this level of wisdom is available to everyone. But we refuse to make time to read God's Word and allow the Holy Spirit to instill its meaning into our lives. There is not a newspaper, television show, or e-mail that can provide more wisdom and guidance in one's life than the Bible. By choosing to never read and study Scripture, one will never gain the level of humility and wisdom that life was meant to have.

The Bible teaches us God's most important standards of measurement for success. Leadership qualities do not come from a résumé, but from faith. Humility is a quality that God so deeply admires and desires for each of us.

One thing my hard lesson in humility uncovered for me is that pleasing the world is not only daunting—at times it is impossible. The world's standards change on a dime. What is important today will be insignificant tomorrow.

However, God's standards never change. What is important to God today has remained constant for thousands of years. Knowing that there is so much more to learn through Him is what cracks our arrogance and builds the foundation for humility. When we persevere to attain humility, the payoff is far greater than anything the world can ever provide in our lives.

We may think being humble makes us appear weak. But actually humility is what gives us integrity and credibility that others will not only find admirable but will also desire to attain for themselves.

Chapter Five

MOTIVATING VS. MANIPULATING

*"Everything is pure to those whose hearts are pure.
But nothing is pure to those who are corrupt and unbelieving, because
their minds and consciences are defiled. Such people claim they know God, but
they deny him by the way they live. They are despicable and disobedient,
worthless for doing anything good."*

TITUS 1:15–16

One of the greatest gifts any individual can have is the ability to motivate, and yet this style of management is often confused with the ability to manipulate. On the surface, it appears these two words have nothing in common. However, what some of us consider motivating strategies are often thinly disguised manipulative tactics.

Motivating means understanding the personal goals of individuals and then applying strategies to help meet the company goals as well as the personal goals of employees.

As discussed previously, a manipulating strategy is when our motive is self-serving and places our personal interests above anything else.

An example of a manipulative tactic is when a new management team is hired and the first thing they do is fire everyone in a particular division. Fear becomes the motivating factor; yet it is used as a manipulative strategy. The assumption is that people will work harder because they fear losing their jobs.

Another manipulating strategy I often experienced in business was the use of threat to get individuals to perform. It was not uncommon for mangers to threaten to take away accounts if salespeople didn't achieve their revenue projections. This tactic is not motivating; it is a manipulative means of showing one's power and authority over others. Although both manipulative strategies may produce results, the motive is for personal gain and will therefore produce only short-term success.

All of us are selfish by nature, and finding leaders who know how to motivate requires serving the needs of others before our own. When I was first promoted into a management position, I never considered my role as a means of serving others. Since people reported to me, wasn't I the one who should be served? The answer is no.

In business, you are only as good as the people you hire. When you hire good people, you get good results. Therefore, managers need to look at their roles as a means of serving their top people and keeping them on the path to success. The only way to successfully accomplish this is to learn what truly motivates each member of the team. Most often the things that motivate people are things that bring personal satisfaction to our lives.

As leaders within our organizations, our strategies for success should be built around meeting both employee and business objectives. Success is achieved when everyone—not just the individuals at the top—wins.

Genuine leaders are the best motivators because their objective is not built on deception and obtaining selfish desires. They uncover strategies of helping others succeed along with the company.

Success will not come from one individual, but from realizing we are only as successful as the team we have in place. Therefore, our goal as leaders within our organizations should be to discover new opportunities that motivate by meeting the personal needs of our employees.

I was in the advertising business most of my career, and economic conditions had a huge impact on sales revenue for the company. If the economy was slow, the first budget our clients cut was advertising. We had no control over the loss of these dollars.

Leaders who are successful motivators develop strategies that allow the company to meet the needs of the salespeople while increasing revenue during the down times.

Instead of cutting commissions and criticizing performance, which are commonly used manipulative tactics, genuine leaders seek advice from top performers and look for opportunities to create a win-win motivating strategy. If salaries need to be cut, it would happen at the top of the organization. This type of leadership style builds loyalty, and employees will be motivated to give 110 percent in their efforts to help the company achieve success.

One of the most motivating leaders written about in the Bible was a man named Nehemiah. It was not his title or position that made him a motivator. Instead, Nehemiah motivated the people of Israel by understanding their needs and what was important to them. Nehemiah was a common, ordinary man. He lived a comfortable life with little power, but became one of the most influential and motivating leaders of biblical times.

For thirteen years after the Israelites returned from captivity in Babylon, the wall around the capital city of Jerusalem was not rebuilt. It had been completely destroyed, leaving the city unguarded from potential attacks. When Nehemiah heard of this, he became very troubled and decided to leave his comfortable life as a servant to the king in Babylon and make it his mission to rebuild this wall around the city.

Many said it was an impossible task. How was Nehemiah going to motivate many individuals he needed to help him with this effort? Building the wall was a daunting task, and one man could not do it alone. Nehemiah had little power, but his leadership qualities provided the level of influence needed to get the task done. Through words of encouragement, he presented this opportunity as a benefit to all of the people of Israel. He organized teams of individuals and instructed them to build the section of the wall that was closest to their homes. The benefit would be that this section would provide protection against enemy attack.

Nehemiah's objective went beyond his personal interests. He blended in his personal goals with the goals of others so that the job became a benefit for everyone involved. Most importantly, Nehemiah also believed his mission was God's purpose and not his own. He prayed for God's direction and help, knowing they would not accomplish this task if God's blessing weren't behind their efforts.

Although enemies continued to threaten them and created obstacles that interfered with its completion, the wall was rebuilt in fifty-two days. Many said this job was too big and could not be done, but Nehemiah knew God was in control, and with God's will, anything was possible.

Nehemiah needed cooperation from every individual who was willing to participate in the reconstruction of the wall. The reward for each individual's efforts was a greater degree of protection for their families and homes. When a reward for the team translates into a personal benefit to everyone involved, motivating a team becomes a simple task and, most importantly, success is attained.

Motivating people is one of the most difficult tasks many leaders face today in the business world. We, as individuals, believe we are in control, so we use our titles as positions of authority to prove to others that we are in control over all matters that affect the company. Many take this control too far, to the point of becoming dictators over their employees. Control becomes a manipulative tactic. The more control we believe we have, the more power we perceive to gain.

This control carries over into every aspect of our lives. We control our families, placing demands on our spouses and children regarding how things need to run in the household. There is no point in voicing an opinion because the opinion of the controller is the only one tolerated. It isn't a matter of what's right or wrong—the opinion of the controller defines what is right and wrong.

I always found it amusing when managers requested opinions from their team, when truthfully the answer had already been predetermined. This happens a lot around budget time. We spent countless hours analyzing projections and spending to forecast our budgets for the upcoming year.

The paperwork that needed to be filled out was massive. And most often, our managers never took the time to review what we had put together. Budgets had already been set.

The exercise became merely a drill for us to go through in reviewing and preparing for the next year. Parts of this exercise carried importance since they were a means to gain a greater understanding of how businesses should run. However, the manner in which it was presented was a manipulative tactic. Bosses had already decided the budgets and were only pretending to seek our opinion on this matter. When we received our budgets, they were entirely different from our business plan. We scratched our heads, wondering why the difference was so great between our plan and our manager's plan.

Every company wants to project an increase in profit for the upcoming year. This keeps investors happy and adds revenue to our bottom line. Instead of having a pre-existing budget plan in place, one of my managers used a motivating strategy with us to help the company achieve its goal. The company was looking for a 10 percent increase over the previous year's billings, and we were asked to put together a strategy of how we could attain this additional 10 percent. If the goal was achieved, we would all receive a specified pre-determined bonus at the end of the year—just in time for the anticipated holiday spending. It was a significant amount of money that everyone saw as a personal benefit to achieve. We worked together as a team to make sure no one fell behind, helping out where needs arose. It was one of the best motivating strategies I had ever experienced in my career.

The difference between these two strategies determines where the control lies within a company. Our boss knew that he couldn't achieve this 10 percent increase without a team that was 100 percent behind the effort. He relinquished his control to those who he knew could make it happen. His function was overseeing the events and moderating areas that needed our attention. It wasn't about taking credit for building a pre-existing plan, but about building a strategy that would be in the best interest of both the company and its employees.

Nehemiah knew in his heart that the success behind rebuilding the wall would not be solely his own. Instead, the project would be successful only by motivating others to meet their personal needs and setting goals so everyone would benefit from the outcome. Most importantly, he prayed about this enormous task in front of him. He knew that ultimately God was in control over all matters in his life and that through faith, anything was possible.

When was the last time we prayed about a matter before deciding its outcome? Do we really believe God has no control over the matters in our office, and more importantly over our lives? Do we live our days believing that we are the sole masters behind our destiny, unwilling to relinquish any level of control over to our Creator? When we choose certain paths in life that take us in a particular direction, we choose to either go with God or go alone. We may claim we are going with God, yet we never pray for His advice.

There are other times we do pray, only to be disappointed with the outcome. This disappointment comes from denying the power of God's will over our lives and all that happens. We want to manipulate the events in our lives in order to achieve what we feel will bring the most personal gain. Yet what we perceive as beneficial may be so much smaller than what God has in store for us down the road.

Having faith does not mean life is free from the bad and ugly events of this world. Often it's the bad and ugly events that have the power to change us from manipulators to motivators. The difference between the two defines where the control exists. Do we think of ourselves as the controllers of all events, willing to manipulate the variables to produce our desired results? Or do we see the impact of turning control over to God and living with unlimited possibilities?

As genuine leaders, we don't aspire for control because we know whatever control we have is smaller than a grain of sand compared to the control God has over our lives. We turn matters over to Him through prayer. Prayer becomes the source of our personal motivation and, most importantly, shows us how to motivate others.

When we look to our jobs as a means of motivating us, it can be disappointing when things happen that are out of our control. Yet, we would rather be miserable than unemployed, so our misery motivates us to show up each day at the office. When we choose particular jobs, we choose to work under particular circumstances. It becomes difficult to tolerate when we look at our jobs as our only means of motivation. We will try to manipulate events at the job to make things better, but often our satisfaction is short-lived.

I worked for an organization whose management often used tactics to control the amount of money their salespeople were able to earn. Our company had just lowered the commission structure as a tactic to motivate the sales team to sell more products. The strategy behind this tactic was that taking away earned income would motivate the team to replace it with new business. Management was concerned we might become too comfortable if we made too much money. It was a manipulative tactic that had adverse results. Instead of motivating us, many salespeople left to find other jobs that paid what they had originally earned.

As managers, we love to control our people and their livelihood, yet the best strategy to motivate our employees is to reward them for their efforts both personally and financially.

Manipulation and motivation are also intertwined at home. We see parents who scream at their children because they believe yelling is the most effective motivating strategy or simply a means of showing who is in control. And I've seen bosses who use these strategies for the same reasons. Does screaming really motivate children toward better behavior or employees to produce better results? Or is personal gain the ultimate behind these manipulative tactics?

When we try to motivate others by control, it becomes personal, and we manipulate the events for our own benefit. You cannot motivate yourself or others when you deny God's presence and control over your life.

Whether our motives are self-serving or to serve others, the determining factor is where we choose to place the control in our lives. Do we turn our goals and decisions over to God, or do we continue to take matters into our own hands? When we accept God's will as the controlling factor in our lives, our actions become motivated by serving Him instead of serving ourselves. Only then can we truly learn what it means to motivate ourselves and others, knowing that our strategies are designed to be a reflection of our faith and will create results leading to success.

Only God is able to read our hearts, and it's our actions that will reveal our true motives. If you have a naturally manipulative style, perhaps God has placed others around you in hopes of changing your heart. Genuine leaders know the ability to motivate comes not from a position of power, but from relinquishing control to our Creator so that our actions become a means of fulfilling His purpose in us for others to see. Faith makes us effective motivators simply by recognizing God's hand in our affairs.

Genuine leaders view their titles as a means of serving, not controlling. They align the company goals with the employees' personal goals. A company is only successful when everyone—not just the leaders at the top—benefits. When we allow our actions to become self serving, success can lead to destruction. This was clearly demonstrated in the fall of Enron. A few individuals at the top became greedy and their needs become more important than the needs of the employees. They used their positions in the company to control the lives of others, and they manipulated their business strategy to obtain more money and power for themselves. This manipulating tactic caused the destruction of the company and of many personal lives.

What type of strategy do we use with our children? Do we motivate them to be the best they can be? Or do we manipulate them to make us as their parents look our best because they achieve what we believe is best for them?

When parents live vicariously through their children, it becomes a matter of trying to manipulate the events in their lives as though the parents had total control over their children's future. However, what often happens is that we force our weaknesses to become perceived strengths for our kids. For instance, most of us were never professional ballplayers, but we push our children to reach this standard before they are ten years old. We demand that our kids have nothing less than straight A's when we went through school with a C average at best.

Our role as parents is to be students of our children in order to understand their innate abilities and interests and then help them develop those areas to the fullest. As genuine leaders, we want to do the same for our employees. A genuine leader would study her team members to see what motivates them and truly care about them on a personal level. Of course, we acknowledge that our children (or employees) have weaknesses and work with them in those areas, too, but we basically "play to their strengths." Do we want to motivate them (our children *and* our employees) to be the best they can be, or do we want to manipulate what their future should be?

Working hard is critical to succeeding in today's world, yet many of us will never know our true talents simply because we have never allowed God into our lives to identify which talents we have. God provides each of us unique gifts that will end up sitting on a shelf, never utilized because we refused to accept the part they play in His sovereign plan. How sad to leave our talents—and those of our children and employees—on the shelf because we don't acknowledge the part they play in accomplishing His will.

Often the path we choose to take in the business world is manipulated by the amount of money we will make rather than the happiness it will bring to our lives. In the beginning, we may find pleasure in our work because of the lifestyle it provides. We think we are motivated by the paycheck when we actually have become manipulated by the status and power it has provided. For me, it was all about the money. In the corporate world, there is a saying that many of us lived by: Show me the money.

When I was asked why I chose a particular career path, my answer was simply that I wanted to make a lot of money. I was a motivated employee and worked very hard to make a good income.

Making money is a necessity to live, but making it our priority can have a disastrous effect on our lives. On the surface, money looks like a motivating factor. But when we look deeper into our hearts, is it really money that is motivating? Or is it the power and control that money provides that makes it a manipulative factor in our hearts?

We desire to live like the rich and famous, and many will go to extremes to make a lot of money despite the harmful effects it can have on our faith and family. We must not be consumed with what money provides, because as easily as it can be obtained, it also has the power to destroy.

Personally, I lost many years away from my family so I could take control of my life, chase the corporate dream and enjoy the income it provided. I can never gain those years back. It is not to say that my corporate life was a bad career choice, but it was not the money that brought value to my life. When we are motivated by the world's standards, we ignore the standards that God provides for us. That indicates we believe we are in control, which is not true—and can also be destructive.

When we follow our faith, God reveals our true motives. He makes it transparent (sometimes painfully) for us to see ourselves through His eyes.

Many of us will never see this because we've decided to build a barrier that keeps God out. But when we allow God in, He will uncover talents we never thought existed. He will reveal the gifts He has instilled in our hearts. He will show us how He has "wired" us and how He can use us. He has the power to motivate us to do things that we never imagined we could accomplish when we leave the choice to Him.

Many of us have the gifted talents of being a CEO, and others have the gifted talents of being a teacher. Whichever career path we choose to take, the success will not come from the money we make, but how we utilize our faith to motivate us each day. When we see our jobs as an opportunity to fulfill God's purpose, there is nothing more motivating than overcoming any obstacles we may face.

Nehemiah clearly recognized God's role in the rebuilding of the wall. The motive behind his desire to see the wall rebuilt was not self-serving. His plan to have it completed was because the wall was a way to protect everyone from possible enemy attacks. Nehemiah never once took credit for rebuilding the wall because he knew it wasn't his talents or level of control that would accomplish this task. He knew it was only God's power and control that would lead to its successful completion. Nehemiah acknowledged that God's purpose in his life was greater than his own. The wall needed to be rebuilt to protect the people, and Nehemiah was chosen by God to accomplish this task.

God knew us before we were born and places our lives in positions to serve His purpose. When we believe that God is in control, it changes our hearts. This change of heart is what transforms our manipulative tactics into a motivating style. When we can see our lives through serving God, we strive to become an example of Christ. We want to motivate others because it is what He expects us to do. We place the needs of others before ourselves, because our personal reward is pleasing God in all that we do. It is this change that results in genuine leadership both at work and at home.

"We can make our plans, but the LORD determines our steps."

PROVERBS 16:9

chapter Six

WHAT'S BEHIND A TITLE?

*"Commit your work to the LORD, and then
your plans will succeed"*

PROVERBS 16:3

As we were pulling up to school one morning, my daughter pointed out a group of girls standing in a circle. She told me those were the "popular" girls at the school and went on to say that this group was often very mean and judgmental. They had the self-ordained power to determine which group a person belongs in: The Popular, The Nerds or The Losers.

I asked her which group she fell into. "I'm either part of the nerdy group, or I guess I'm a loser," she answered. My heart sank as I observed how she identified her significance by a title that someone else had given her. Yet, as adults we are no different in the way we define others and ourselves by the titles we wear.

You have an important title. Does your position entitle you to be first within your company? Jesus once shared with His disciples,

"But many who seem to be important now will be the least important then, and those who are considered least here will be the greatest then."

MARK 10:31

I love the story in the Bible about the disciples who argued amongst themselves which of them was the greatest. Jesus responded,

"Anyone who wants to be the first must take last place and be the servant of everyone else."

MARK 9:35

The conversation with my daughter stayed on my mind throughout the day. It made me think about what group Jesus must have belonged to while He walked on this earth. He certainly wasn't part of the "popular" group since this group had Him crucified. Therefore, I suppose He would have been placed in either the nerdy or loser group. In fact, if we consider the people that He chose to be His disciples, they were probably in one of those latter groups also.

Peter was a fisherman
Matthew was a despised tax collector
James was a fisherman
John was a fisherman
Andrew was a fisherman
Philip was a fisherman
Bartholomew–unknown
Thomas–unknown
James–unknown
Thaddaeus–unknown
Simon the Zealot–unknown
Judas Iscariot–unknown

None of these men had power or authority by the world's standards, yet Jesus saw them as the most influential individuals to help Him personally carry out His mission.

Today, our titles in the corporate world determine everything from who we spend our time with to the size of office we occupy. I have to honestly admit that one aspect I loved about corporate America was that the bigger the title I had, the more perks I received.

When I was first promoted into management, I recall how excited it was to receive a nice-sized office, a personal secretary and a convenient parking space. I also had an unlimited expense account, which allowed me to dine at some of the most fabulous restaurants around the country. In my mind, life couldn't get any better.

It was also amazing how quickly I became more popular as a top executive than I had been as a salesperson. Friends instantly seemed to fall out of nowhere. I was on top of the world, all because of a new title that carried so much weight and importance in my life.

Then, one day, it was taken from me. Our company went through a merger, and suddenly our titles were stripped from us. The positions that were once considered important were no longer needed. I remember feeling devastated by this event and was suddenly faced with the fear of unknown significance. I will never forget that first morning of being unemployed, staring at my children and our nanny and wondering where I fit in. My title with the company had defined my own existence, more than the title of motherhood God had provided me.

I couldn't imagine not putting on a suit, heading into my office for meetings and running the day's business operations. Everything else in my life had always taken a back row seat to my work, including my family and my faith. After so many years of a fast-paced career, identifying my importance by the title I held there, staying home suddenly made me feel like I was in a foreign country.

Financially, both my husband and I needed to work to support the lifestyle we had established. However, my choice of work was based not only on money, but also on opportunities for me to grow professionally, despite the challenges of motherhood as we raised two children.

My sister once told me that I couldn't have it all—that something would suffer. But I believed I could have it all, and nothing would be left behind. I quickly learned that the two most important aspects of my life—family and faith—had been left behind. I never once considered God's role in my life because I was too preoccupied with my own success. The quality of my life was defined by what I owned, and not by what I believed. It was all about me.

Titles have existed since the beginning of man. They define our socioe-conomic status in this world, placing individuals in rank of importance.

When we hear a person's title, what image or stereotype do we form in our minds about that individual? We can't deny the fact that we judge people based on their titles. A bigger title often means greater significance. A lesser title often means less significance. That's how the corporate world defines our importance. Sad to say, we have become so disillusioned by this dogma that we now measure ourselves by the same standards regarding our importance in this world. We look at our titles as a way to measure ourselves against others and define our purpose in life.

The illusion is that the bigger the title we have, the more we have to personally gain. Smaller titles may not be worthy of our valuable time. In the corporate world, leaders place such significance on their titles that everything else becomes secondary. Even one's time becomes too valuable to spend with those several layers beneath them.

In many cases, new employees get hired and never even see the face of the person who runs the office. The end result is that leaders don't even know the individuals who help make their company successful. Contributions become more important than the names of the individuals who made them. We call ourselves leaders, but we don't even take the time to know our own employees.

What does this say about corporate leadership today? Have we become so puffed up with prideful titles, that we limit our communication to e-mails and a few direct reports? How can a company today have core values when we can't even find the time to interact with those who are contributing to our success?

We all know bosses who stay in their offices all day. In one company I worked for, the only time I saw the bosses leave their offices was when they went to get coffee or use the bathroom. Of course, this kind of boss says he has an open-door policy and that anyone is welcome to come and share what's on their mind.

Truthfully, how often do employees that don't directly report to you come into your office to even say hello? If you have never taken the time to step out of your office and visit with your people, they will never feel at ease speaking with you. How is one able to motivate and lead a team if we don't take the time to know their personal goals and objectives? You can certainly manipulate people you don't know, but it is impossible to motivate those you've never met.

When you read the stories found in the first four books of the New Testament in the Bible, it is amazing to consider the amount of time Jesus gave to those around Him. He holds the most significant title in our world, yet His title never got in the way of being too busy or too important to serve multitudes of people who gathered around Him to be healed and hear His teachings.

How tired He must have felt as he walked from city to city, sharing His words with those who would listen. Although His disciples sometimes tried to insulate Him, He never once said, "I'm too important to spend time with all of these people." He gave every moment He physically could to anyone who was willing to accept Him. His motive was not to be served, but to serve others by showing them a way of life that would lead to salvation.

Conversations with employees should focus on uncovering personal goals and personal needs. If you claim to have an open-door policy for individuals to come in and share ideas and challenges, this is an important step. Motivating your team will require having this information so that your strategy for success benefits both the company and your employees. When people feel their personal objectives are being considered, everyone wins.

Today, however, the significance we place on our titles may be creating a barrier of trust between our employees and us. If people feel intimidated by our titles, the level of trust needed to effectively lead a team will be non-existent. Employees will tell us only what they feel we want to hear. What could potentially be a constructive, informative meeting will become nothing more than a flattery session when we meet with our team. Conversations between all levels within an organization should never be negative. Instead, they should create an opportunity for everyone to freely and openly provide their input on important business matters.

As leaders, we must remove our titles and listen with our hearts, not allowing our arrogance to slip in and cause us to be judgmental. Listening with our heart provides valuable insight. Praying about our decision creates opportunities for success.

When Nehemiah supervised the rebuilding of the wall surrounding Jerusalem, there were individuals who felt their titles and significance were above participating in the reconstruction process. In fact, many of them even criticized this initiative, claiming it could never be done.

I've witnessed sales managers with similar attitudes. They felt they had paid their dues, and therefore no longer participated in working with clients, bringing new business to the company, or getting to know those who were lower in rank. Their titles had puffed them up with pride and they disassociated themselves from anything or anyone they felt was beneath them.

When this attitude surfaces among the different levels of management, the cohesiveness of the team begins to deteriorate. Titles become a weapon for status and attention. Manipulation is the hidden motive behind this kind of leader's actions and the leader takes credit for things others have accomplished, basically using a titles to gain power and authority. Leadership becomes self-serving, and motivating a team becomes an impossible task. A title doesn't create a leader. Genuine leadership stems from one's faith, which places other's needs before our own and recognizes God's hand in the process.

Never once in the story of Nehemiah do we hear of him being critical of the work being done, nor did he ever place his needs above others. People were grateful for his initiative when they saw it as a personal benefit. Nehemiah's words were always encouraging, and he never once took credit for the successes. Nor did he expect gratitude for the completion of the wall.

He had to motivate hundreds of individuals and assign each person specific tasks. Some individuals had the role of protecting the workers against enemies who were threatening to attack. Others were responsible for bringing supplies. The focus was not on titles and ranks of importance, but on the objective at hand. God used Nehemiah for His purpose, and Nehemiah relied on God to help him accomplish this mission. If the reconstruction were handled any other way, the wall would never have been completed. Nehemiah is a nice model for any business to follow in today's world.

Companies assign us titles that place us in a chain of command. I recall one company that sent out a monthly flow chart, reflecting this chain of command so that everyone could see who they reported to by title and rank. Management structure is critical to a company's success, but when we allow our titles to define our purpose and existence, our actions become self-serving. Our egos tell us we don't need God because everything so far has run smoothly without Him.

Have we become so blinded that we believe we alone are the result of our successes, and that our title is our proof on paper that reflects our level of success? Do titles get us into heaven? Does a title indicate favoritism by God?

"My dear brothers and sisters, how can you claim that you have faith in our glorious Lord Jesus Christ if you favor some people more than others?"

JAMES 2:1

God does not care about titles, nor are they the ticket to salvation. God looks for qualities in one's heart. Moses, a poor shepherd, was chosen by God to lead the people of Israel out of Egypt. David, a poor shepherd and musician, became one of the greatest kings ever. Our significance in God's eyes is not found in a title, but in the depth of our faith. So if God is capable of looking beyond a title, what makes it so difficult for us to do so? Why did I feel so lost once my title was stripped away? A common dilemma we face is deciding whose favor we seek more: God's or man's.

On the surface, we are quick to answer this question. How could we possibly seek the approval of others over God's approval of us? We claim our Christian faith and attend services every Sunday morning. We occasionally read the Bible, and perhaps have even participated in a Bible study, yet our actions show where our true allegiance lies. We live in a materialistic world and we desire materialistic things. When we show favoritism toward others because they have a certain lifestyle we desire to attain, our love for this world and its ultimate approval becomes greater than our love for God and our seeking His favor.

Are we even capable of recognizing God's favor in our lives? For me, my significance stemmed from my title, and seeking the approval from my bosses became more important than God's approval of me. We seek favoritism from those with bigger titles and bigger incomes, and fail to recognize God's favoritism and significance in our own lives.

"Don't try to get rich by extortion or robbery. And if your wealth increases, don't make it the center of your life."

PSALM 62:10

Wealth and prestige have become our means of measuring one's significance, but God's way of measuring us is dependent on our faith alone and serving Him above everything else in our lives. He favors those who recognize His power and authority, making Him the center of one's existence.

We don't deserve God's favor, but He provides it to us anyway. The fact that God is even willing to forgive us for all that we have done is a sign of favoritism. Each day we have on this earth is a sign of favoritism from God. When we begin to take His favor for granted, we lose sight of all that He is in our lives, and all that He hopes for us to become.

"LORD, remind me how brief my time on earth will be. Remind me that my days are numbered, and that my life is fleeing away. My life is no longer than the width of my hand. An entire lifetime is just a moment to you; human existence is but a breath."

PSALM 39:4–5

Pride creates self-driven measures for success, which often take us down a different path from our faith. What is important to God is that we place Him over everything else in our lives. He disapproves of everything that is placed before Him, including our pride.

The one thing that should be behind a title is a person who sees their position as serving a much greater importance than what the job description provides. God uses all of us to fulfill His purpose despite what group the world has placed us in. When we can see ourselves from God's perspective, our purpose becomes far greater that what is printed on a business card.

chapter seven

WHEN PRIDE CROSSES THE LINE

*"Enjoy prosperity while you can.
But when hard times strike, realize that both come from God.
That way you will realize that nothing is certain in this life."*

ECCLESIASTES 7:14

Pride is an interesting quality. It fuels our self-worth and helps to build confidence. It's important to take pride in our accomplishments. We strive to work hard and be our best, and the pride we have in the final outcome can be rewarding. I love it when my children say, "watch me," or "look at this." They're proud of their work, and receiving praise often becomes more important than the work itself. Pride is an important quality, and if kept in a proper perspective, it can become a motivating factor behind one's success. The challenge we face is identifying when it has become too much. What happens when our pride crosses the line and changes from building our confidence to creating arrogance—an air of superiority? It's a fine line for many, and one that is easily crossed if not kept in check.

Many of us have heard the story from the Bible about David and Goliath. When we think of David, the story that comes to mind is the image of a young man who defeats and kills a giant-sized man named Goliath.

David was a powerful warrior, and years later, he became a great king over Israel.

In the beginning of King David's reign, he was victorious in every battle and situation he confronted. The people believed he truly was a man of God, and initially it was his faith and loyalty to God that brought him so much success. His accomplishments as a musician, poet, warrior and king were certainly ones to be proud of. But David's pride eventually crossed the line.

The longer he was king, the more power and wealth he was given. His dependence on God began to fade. Eventually, David's primary purpose was not pleasing God first, but fulfilling his own personal desires.

David was at the top of his game when he committed adultery and murder. He committed adultery with a woman who was someone else's wife. When she reported to David that she was pregnant with his child, he then arranged to have her husband killed so he could marry her with few questions asked.

Eventually, David was overthrown as king. And for some time, he lived his life running from the circumstances that stemmed from a prideful spirit. When all was going well in David's life, God's priorities faded in their importance to him. His pride crossed the line when he got caught up in his own power and splendor.

Pride has the ability to destroy if taken too far. It is our pride that wants to call all of the shots and have complete control over the events of our lives. People who allow pride to cross the line can cause so much damage to an organization simply by the words they use and actions they take as a means of boosting their own self-esteem.

For many, status and socioeconomic status become the instigators behind a prideful heart. Have we ever considered whether God had anything to do with the position we hold in a company, or the amount of money we have in our bank accounts? Did we obtain all that we have by our own efforts? God knew us before we were born. Have we become so proud that we think our Creator had nothing to do with any of our accomplishments?

Our pride can mislead us when taken too far. When we identify ourselves by the world's standards, we find ourselves competing by the world's standards. Keeping up with the Joneses becomes more important than keeping up with our faith. We need to stop for a moment and ask ourselves, *What expectations does God have for me today?* That will keep our pride from crossing the line to becoming boastful. God has a way of changing our hearts from: "It's all about me," to, "It's *not* all about me."

I started writing this book while I was working in a corporate environment. As I was growing stronger in my faith, I began seeing myself for the first time as a stranger in a world where I had been so connected to my whole life. Over the years, my heart had hardened to events that suddenly started to bother me. The criticism and deception that lives in the business world was affecting me both physically and emotionally.

It wasn't that the environment was any different from previous companies, but my perspective had changed. What I thought I was supposed to be in the business world became drastically different than the purpose God had for me in this position. I began to see criticism and deception as manipulative tactics used every day in business. I could no longer turn my head the other way and convince myself that these practices were simply the norm of the business world.

It became clear that God was making things uncomfortable for me. I thought I had the perfect job, and at the time, I thought I would be there for many years. However, as my pride began to diminish, my perspective changed from the "me" in my life to "Him."

When we look at our adversity through God's eyes, it changes the way we respond. My pride told me to "put up or shut up" with what was happening at work. My ego said to be angry and bitter toward those who were affecting my future. However, when I was able to see God's presence and purpose in the midst of my anger, there was suddenly no room for bitterness.

Perhaps one of the reasons God allows for trials in our lives is to diminish our pride and make us more dependent on Him. I had to live through the adversity to see His purpose and control over my life. God plays a role in every aspect of our lives, including business. Until we acknowledge that fact, pride will continue to cross the line.

"When I was prosperous I said, 'Nothing can stop me now!'
Your favor, O LORD, made me as secure as a mountain.
Then you turned away from me, and I was shattered."

PSALM 30:6–7

We are no different than King David. We can be at the top of our career when we experience our greatest fall. It's easy, yet very dangerous, to get caught up in the things of this world. Although it will seem like our materialism can satisfy our every need, something will always feel like it's missing when our purpose is self-serving.

Despite how horrible David's sin was in God's eyes, David held in his heart a quality that many of us can easily overlook, especially when we are at the top of our game.

FEAR

David had lost everything. He lost his power. He lost his family and most importantly, he lost his dignity. However, it wasn't the fear of losing everything that changed David from a prideful heart to a humble spirit. It was David's fear of God. It became greater than anything else in his life. Receiving God's forgiveness was more important than losing all that he had obtained on this earth. Repentance filled his broken heart, and David was able to accept God's hand in both the successes and failures of his life.

David could have become bitter and resentful toward God. It would have been easier to blame others for his fall than to accept his own negligence. However, David's pride was replaced by humility and he could see God's presence in his adversities.

When pride crosses the line, it evaporates our fear of God. The more pride we have, the less we feel our need for Him. We take matters into our own hands, believing we have all the answers. Why is there a need to involve God, especially when things are going so well? A prideful spirit convinces us that the fear of losing all that we have is far greater than our fear of God, especially when He points out and speaks to our hearts, using the words: "Let Me show you what you could have done."

A prideful heart can drown out our need for faith. However, repentance cannot come from a prideful heart, but from a humble spirit that sees that all we have and all we represent are blessings from Him.

"For I recognize my shameful deeds—they haunt me day and night. Against you and you alone, have I sinned; I have done what is evil in your sight. You will be proved right in what you say, and your judgment against me is just."

PSALM 51:3–4

This was David's plea to God. The challenge we face is that often our pleas only come when things are going bad in our lives. Why would there be a need to pray to God when all is good?

It is in these moments that we build a false sense of security, believing nothing bad will ever happen. We wake up in the morning, drive to our offices, conduct our meetings, attend dinner engagements, and live our life accordingly. We get caught up in the mundane routines, not realizing that what we consider mundane is actually a blessing from God. A prideful heart makes it easy to overlook God's blessings of a normal routine day and the significance it can have in our life.

Things can change in an instant, and although we aren't able to understand all that is happening in our lives, we can rest assured that God never abandons us. When we pray and ask for God's help, He graciously provides—once we are able to surrender our pride to Him.

Our sinful nature causes us to have a prideful heart that continues to feed our sinful ways. It is our pride that takes us further from our faith. God is under no obligation to forgive us, but He chooses to forgive those who come to repent with a humble and broken spirit at all moments—good and bad—in our lives.

If we go on living our lives without praying for God's guidance, can we really identify where our allegiance truly lies? Perhaps our fear of man is greater than our fear of God and the consequences He will someday place before us.

From God's perspective, there is no smaller sin or greater sin. Sin is sin, and a prideful heart causes us to place all He has provided us above our dependence on Him.

Stop allowing pride to cross the line and fill your ego with the misconception that God is not actively working in every aspect of your life. He has everything to do with where you are today, and only He knows for certain where you will be tomorrow.

Chapter Eight

WHEN TERMINATION BECOMES OUR REWARD

"This suffering is all part of what God has called you to.
Christ, who suffered for you is your example. Follow his steps.
He never sinned, and he never deceived anyone. He did not retaliate when
he was insulted. When he suffered, he did not threaten to get even.
He left his case in the hands of God, who always judges fairly."

1 PETER 2:21-23

I f you have ever been fired from a job, you know how devastating it can feel. Perhaps you had a boss whose expectations were exceedingly difficult to reach. Sometimes a termination is not based on individual performance but it happens because of a change in the way business is conducted. A change in compensation can force people to leave, or even a change in what the company feels is important. The company's vision has changed since the day you were hired and you feel out of place.

For example, there are companies that shy away from hiring anyone over 50. Their culture is primarily made up of employees 35 years of age and younger, although legally, they can't admit it. But when all of the young new hires begin flooding the workplace, one wonders what impact that will have on the older employees. Laws have made it harder for companies to fire employees who don't fit the corporate culture because they know they could face discriminatory lawsuits. What often happens is that companies will make the job so difficult that people will quit simply because they feel defeated and discouraged.

When one does get terminated, our pride tells us we didn't deserve this treatment. We are better than the bosses who fired us. Whether we deserved it or not, our resentment can become the obstacle that prevents us from moving forward in our lives. We begin to make mental lists of all the people we feel have wronged us. Our pride builds a wall, preventing us from pursuing the next opportunity. Whatever the case may be, when we harbor anger in our hearts, we are heading down a path of negativity and possibly destruction. Moving forward and picking up the pieces of one's life can be a grueling and painful process.

I have never been fired from a company, but I certainly have felt like I've been pushed toward the door to the point of having my resignation forced on me. I accepted a job with a lesser title that allowed me more time and flexibility to be with my family. By the world's standards, it was a demotion. However, my priorities for my career had changed when my faith revealed there was more to a job than titles and big offices. I loved to work, but I had a greater love to be a mother. This new position, one that I had prayed for, appeared to provide me the balance to have the best of both worlds.

A new manager came in and took over our division. In a very short time, over half of our staff had either resigned or been terminated. It was clear this person was looking to bring in her own team of people. I could have easily resented her for what she was doing. But when we place our faith first in our lives, God uses both the bad and good to reveal His plan for us. He plays a role in our successes just as His hand plays a role in our struggles. God showed me that what appeared to be the perfect job was only a stepping- stone to becoming stronger in my faith.

I always knew in the back of my mind that I would leave corporate America, but I never dreamed it would happen the way that it did. I recall the day I walked out. I thought about changing my mind for fear over my family's financial livelihood, but God had a different plan for me. I remember a coworker approaching me that day, expressing her disbelief in how things had transpired. The words from my mouth still surprise me today. "Don't be mad about this. God did it." Her smiled confirmed that I was right. This adversity was about to open a new door in my life, although I couldn't see it at the time. I was afraid about what tomorrow would hold, but something told me that I was to trust Him.

Our fears that come from our struggles can paralyze us. When we believe that our destinies are in the hands of this world, we become narrow in our thinking. We ask ourselves over and over again, *How will I go on? What's going to happen now?* These are real questions that we face, and when we can't see the solution in front of us, often we fall into a state of depression. There is only one who can see into our future. He knows exactly where we're headed. The choice becomes how we're going to get there. We can choose to face our adversity with faith, or without.

In the Book of Genesis, there is story of a man named Joseph who provides one of the most powerful examples of an individual looking at the struggles in his life as a divine moment to be seized.

Joseph was the son of a man named Jacob. In fact, he was his father's favorite son. This favoritism led to his brothers' resentment and jealousy of him, resulting in their throwing him into a hole in hopes he would die. However, they didn't want to live with a guilty conscience, so they took the opportunity to sell him to a passing caravan. Joseph was then taken to Egypt and sold to Potiphar, a member of the personal staff of Pharaoh, the king of Egypt. Potiphar eventually gave Joseph the responsibility of watching over his entire household as well as his business dealings.

The Bible describes Joseph as being very handsome. Potiphar's wife falsely accused him of attempting to rape her. The truth was that she wanted to have an affair with Joseph, but when he refused, she lied and told her husband that Joseph tried to rape her. Her lie caused Joseph to be thrown in prison, forgotten by the outside world. During his time in prison, Joseph met the king's cupbearer and interpreted a dream that the cupbearer had shared with him. The dream actually came true and the cupbearer was eventually released and returned to his palace duties. Joseph had asked the cupbearer to remind Pharaoh of him, but once again, Joseph was forgotten for two years.

All the while he was in prison, and after all that had happened, Joseph never reflected on the events in his life with anger or resentment. His brothers tried to kill him, Potiphar's wife had him wrongfully thrown into jail, and the cupbearer forgot about him. Yet, he accepted these adversities with strength and a positive attitude, knowing in his heart that God had a purpose in his life and would use both Joseph's successes and trials to do His work.

In our business life, God's presence is rarely acknowledged, but He is very active. Our pride tells us that getting even with those who have wronged us is the best course of action. Some may even go to extreme measures to accomplish this. However, when we allow God in, it becomes clear how He places certain people in our lives for His purpose and not our own.

One night, Pharaoh had two dreams and no one was able to tell him what they meant. The cupbearer remembered Joseph and his ability to interpret dreams. He told Pharaoh about Joseph and what had happened to him while he was in prison.

Pharaoh ordered Joseph's release and asked him to provide the meaning behind the dreams. Joseph told Pharaoh that he didn't have the power to do this, but admitted the power was from God. He successfully interpreted Pharaoh's dream and was eventually made ruler over Egypt.

Pharaoh's dreams had been about Egypt enjoying seven years of prosperity and then facing seven years of famine. Just as Joseph had predicted, the events came true.

During the years of famine, Joseph's brothers came to Egypt in search of food. Joseph recognized them immediately. It had been twenty years since his brothers had tried to kill him. A prideful heart would have remembered with bitterness the events of that day. A prideful heart would have held resentment and mentally made a list of the punishment they so rightfully deserved.

Joseph was different. He was not a proud man. Resentment cannot exist when we look at our problems as a means for God to fulfill His purpose. After revealing himself to his brothers, he said to them,

> *"But don't be angry with yourselves that you did this to me, for God did it."*

GENESIS 45:5

Joseph didn't recite all of the terrible things that had happened and remind his brothers how badly they had treated him. Instead, he accepted that the reasoning behind his brothers' actions were all a part of God's plan.

What does it take before we are able to look at challenges in our lives as possible stepping-stones in our faith? How do we mentally erase those mental lists in our minds of the individuals whom we feel have betrayed us? Eventually, this list leads us to a life of bitterness that eats away at our hearts. I had lunch with a former coworker who was still angry over what she believed had been her forced resignation, orchestrated by her boss. Two years had passed, and she still had feelings of resentment. We can never move forward until we get rid of all of the baggage that has collected past feelings of resentment in our lives. It weighs us down.

The scriptures tell us we are never to allow resentment to enter our hearts in the first place. In fact, the question becomes: "Can God truly forgive us if we cannot forgive others." The answer is no. As long as we hold our resentment, God withholds His grace from our lives.

"If you forgive those who sin against you, your heavenly Father will forgive you. But if you refuse to forgive others, your Father will not forgive your sins."

MATTHEW 6:14–15

My coworker finally succumbed to prayer, asking God for direction in her career path and letting go of her anger. She didn't want to be mad, but until she could feel His presence in her life, the resentment continued to linger.

When we feel God's purpose in our lives, we can look at our struggles and adversities as a means of growing in our faith and opening the door to new opportunities. Often it is the adversities we experience that build our level of endurance. My coworker eventually got a new job that provided her the financial support as well as more flexibility to be at home for her children. This new career ended up being better than her previous job. Turning our adversities over to God eliminates our resentment and will direct us down a brighter and more rewarding path.

When we see our importance as tied strictly to a title and paycheck, leaving a job for whatever reason will be a difficult obstacle to overcome. It means we see our purpose from the world's standards and often miss what God has in mind. Losing a job is not a bad thing if we can look at it as a means of growing in our faith. Perhaps getting fired is actually a blessing in disguise.

When we decide change is too scary to face, we must be prepared because God may force this change whether we think we're ready or not. He does this because He loves us. Our resistance to change and leaving our comfort zone may be what's preventing us from living the life He so desperately wants for us. My prayer to God became: "Help me be what You need me to be."

When you pray for this, be careful. You might just get what you prayed for. I lost my job. My family lost a level of income. I lost my "perceived significance." I worried about how the bills would get paid. And every day, I thanked God for all that He did.

Turning our problems over to God opens our hearts to new and better opportunities, and most importantly, we begin to define ourselves by a higher standard. For Joseph, the end result from his struggles resulted in God saving his entire family from starving to death during those years of famine. Had things happened differently, his family may have died.

Getting fired is never easy, but discovering a new purpose beyond the walls of an office building can be our greatest reward. Often, it is the adversities that God hopes will bring us closer to Him. There is no room for anger and bitterness when we can see life and everything that is thrown at us as a means of becoming stronger in our relationship with God. It doesn't mean things will become easy, but it does mean that no matter what happens we can survive, knowing God is in control.

Chapter Nine

WHY PEOPLE LEAVE

*"People who accept correction are on the pathway to life, but
those who ignore it will lead others astray."*

PROVERBS 10:17

There are many cases when terminating an employee is the best solution for both parties. However, in today's corporate world, we experience far more turnover of employees than we did forty years ago. It was not uncommon for our grandparents—and perhaps our parents— to have been employed with one company their entire working life. The picture is much different today. Statistically, five years is the average time span an individual spends with one company; and in some industries, it is much less. What has happened in the corporate culture to cause such an increase in turnover?

In one company I worked for, my manager lost twenty salespeople in one year. She had a total of thirty-five on her staff, so the turnover represented over half of the team. What was even more peculiar about this was that the president who oversaw the operations of our office never seemed noticed all of the people leaving. As far as he was concerned, as long as budgets were being made, things were operating normally.

higher income to a new hire. Rather, it's often more preferable to hire individuals with limited or no experience because they cost less in the short term.

What are the most important qualities companies want today from potential candidates? My experience in hiring salespeople had me looking for individuals who were aggressive, assertive, and willing to do whatever it took to succeed. We simply hired individuals to fill desks because the more desks that were filled, the greater the chances of sales being made.

This is a common tactic used today by many companies and it often becomes the reason most people leave. Personal expectations are never met from either side of the table. The maxim could be stated: We don't hire the best; we settle for what little we are willing to invest.

However, despite the level of salary a company guarantees, we learn quickly that money isn't always the motivating factor for staying. People will leave jobs when things start to get really bad, regardless of size of the paycheck they leave behind.

When people resign, the first thing we, as leaders, should consider is where we went wrong. However, in today's business world, we fail at this task simply by never admitting we may have been the problem. Hiring people becomes a manipulative tactic because we hire based on what we feel will make us look best and not on what is actually best for the company, and more importantly for our customers.

When we are able to look beyond the qualities we desire and consider those that are most desired by God, success will come beyond the revenue one brings to the bottom line. I once hired a salesperson nearly twenty years older than myself. Honestly, I must admit that his age was a concern of mine. In the Internet business, our company typically hired young candidates, right out of school, or with a minimum of two years in sales.

When this gentleman came for his interview, I asked him directly why he would want to work at this level when his experience far exceeded what the position had to offer. He shared with me that the Internet was an intriguing medium and he felt his background with traditional media would be one of the greatest assets he could bring to this job.

He knew the advantages and disadvantages of every possible advertising medium, and expressed candidly that anyone who didn't have this expertise would be far less valuable to clients in helping them achieve their marketing initiatives. Something inside told me to hire this man, despite the additional costs our department would incur by hiring someone at this level. I took the chance and must say that he was one of the best salespeople I have ever worked with. He had been in management previously and knew the challenges I faced on a daily basis. Not only was he a huge help to me, he also became a wonderful mentor to the team.

The qualities this man carried were not the standard qualities that we, as sales managers, admired. He exemplified the list of genuine qualities the apostle Paul wrote about to Titus. There was nothing assertive about him. In fact, he was one of the most humble human beings I have ever met. In a very short period of time, he became one of the company's top performers.

God brings people into our lives for a reason. Perhaps this was God's way of showing me to listen with my heart and look deeper for qualities that represent a much higher standard. Often God uses others to help those who are lost. I was lost in God's eyes, and perhaps this gentleman was an instrument to reflect the true qualities that God desires of me.

God works diligently to change our hearts, and He uses others to help Him accomplish this mission. By denying His involvement in our lives, we deny Him, and our pride blinds us to any other possible rationale behind the reason given for one's resignation.

"The LORD has made everything for his own purposes, even the wicked for punishment."

PROVERBS 16:4

He uses us in moments like these to knock down the barriers of pride that we've built around our hearts. My pride could have prevented me from hiring this person for fear that he might take my job. Our pride tells us never to hire people better than ourselves, yet God instructs in His Word that we are to look at everyone as being better than ourselves.

God uses others to force us to listen with our hearts and open our eyes so that we can see clearly what is going on around us. God wants to tear down the wall we've built between our jobs and our faith and apply the same values at work as we do Sunday mornings at church. When we turn to God for His hand in our matters, opportunities for fulfillment and prosperity await us. God opens our minds to acknowledge that the role we play in our jobs is either a reflection of Him or an image of a prideful heart.

"You know that in this world kings are tyrants, and officials lord over the people beneath them. But among you it should be quite different. Whoever wants to be a leader among you must be your servant, and whoever wants to be first must be the slave of all. For even I, the Son of Man, came here not to be served but to serve others, and to give my life as a ransom for many."

MARK 10:42–45).

Companies have personalities based on the characteristics associated with them. Some companies are known for their quality of service and honorable means of doing business. Others carry the reputation of being egotistical, focused solely on profit and gain over customer service. What are the characteristics of your company? How does the market perceive you in the way business is conducted?

When compromising business practices are allowed to exist, it defines one's true qualities. When greed, money and power are the true motives, the absence of character paves the road to disaster. Companies need to make money, but not at the expense of sacrificing the company's personal integrity and character. People leave when their credibility becomes threatened. A manager who only sees her employees as a body that fills a desk will never gain respect and loyalty.

For some, money is the only factor behind keeping a job. Others desire much more out of their work and want the job to provide an environment that focuses on aligning the needs of the employees with the goals of the company.

Managers have a way of driving people out by subjecting them to heated pressure to perform above and beyond the stated expectations. Hitting revenue goals is no longer enough for one to keep their job. Employees are required to go above and beyond company expectations to justify their existence. When the basis for success is solely based on efficiency and productivity, people become unhappy and they leave.

In one company I worked with, as long as you showed up at 8:30 every morning, never left the office before 5:30 P.M., and hit your monthly budget, you were considered a top performer. The question one must ask is: "Will this bring happiness to the job?"

For me, the answer was no. I needed to feel there was more to my career than a nine-hour workday and a paycheck provided at the end of the month.

The feeling behind true success comes only from fulfillment, seeing the value of our contributions beyond the functions of the daily operations. When we no longer feel that the job is fulfilling, we become unhappy and search elsewhere.

Perhaps you're in a similar dilemma. Your work lacks fulfillment and has become nothing more than a financial obligation. It is solely a means of paying the bills and living at a certain socioeconomic status. Yet, the days seem empty and robotic. The work has become a distraction, or perhaps even an escape from your life at home. How do we get to this point in our lives, and more importantly, how do we get out? We can always look for new jobs, but even this offers no guarantee of fulfillment.

The choice we have to make is to continue down this path without God or to consider a new path that brings Him along with us. This may have been the job you prayed for, but after getting it, you realized God was no longer a part of your day. When we keep God excluded from our days, we can't experience fulfillment. God has placed you in this position for a reason, yet His reason goes beyond providing the financial means of support. What you perceive to be unfulfilling may actually be an opportunity to work in the lives of others for God's purpose.

When we feel heaviness and discouragement from our jobs, we turn to those in the office who always reflect a positive image. Have you ever watched how people gravitate to those who are kind and upbeat despite the daily challenges they face? This is what we become when we acknowledge

God's presence in our lives. He shows us the way to face obstacles as divine moments. He gives us encouragement to handle any crisis.

I often found myself praying before I entered the building of my office so that each day would give me a sense of peace. My office was filled with harsh words, arrogance and criticism from individuals at all levels. Yet, my faith showed me that God placed me in the midst of this environment to reflect His strength and kindness as well as encouragement for those whose integrity had been attacked.

When I felt God wasn't present in the office, He would immediately bring a Christian coworker alongside me and use that person to encourage me. When we allow God into our lives, we can see beyond the office negativity and rely on our faith as the means to encourage others in an environment where kindness is typically not welcomed.

Often, the negativity that initially presents itself as a problem becomes a divine moment for us to experience. How many times have we become victims of a personal attack that is completely unjustified? Perhaps God may be using us as a reflection of Him in the way we handle ourselves in particular situations.

Whatever reason you give for your departure, pray that you will handle your resignation the way God would expect. If you're a manager experiencing high turnover, pray for discernment and guidance in becoming the leader that He intended for you to be.

God uses our hearts to guide our actions and approach every situation with the highest level of integrity for His purpose. When we are able to get to this point, we find the grass couldn't possibly be any greener than the pasture we are standing in right now.

"So don't worry about having enough food or drink or clothing. Why be like the pagans who are so deeply concerned about these things? Your heavenly Father already knows all your needs, and he will give you all you need from day to day if you live for him and make the Kingdom of God your primary concern."

MATTHEW 6:31–33

Chapter Ten

SERVING VS. MANAGING

*"Cry out for insight and understanding. Search for them
as you would for lost money or hidden treasure.
Then you will understand what it means to fear the LORD, and
you will gain knowledge of God. For the LORD grants wisdom!
From his mouth come knowledge and understanding.
He grants a treasure of good sense to the godly.
He is their shield, protecting those who walk with integrity.
He guards the paths of justice and protects those who are faithful to him."*

PROVERBS 2: 3–8

Israel's first king was a man named Saul. By the world's standards, Saul appeared to have the qualities to lead a nation. Although God had warned the people about the danger of turning away from Him and relying on others for guidance, the people of Israel so badly wanted to be like other nations who had kings. God gave into their demands and appointed Saul as their new leader.

However, it wasn't long after Saul was pronounced king before his arrogance and pride took over his heart. He became more focused on being in the limelight than in serving God who placed him in this position in the first place. Saul was the type of leader who reacted impulsively in making decisions and often took credit for successes he did not deserve. Needless to say, his reign became a disaster for the nation. Saul's failure resulted from turning his back on his spiritual faith.

For many of us, the concept of serving in lieu of managing is incomprehensible. We have a title; therefore, others should serve us. We were the ones promoted; therefore, we have all of the expertise. Why would we look at our position as a means of serving our faith? This mindset is what exists in the corporate world today, and because of it we miss God's calling for us to be more than simply a manager.

How does one successfully hear God's calling to serve? The first step is to relinquish your control to Him and seek His advice on all matters. Genuine leaders seek advice from individuals at all levels because they allow God to work in their hearts, without regard to position. Titles don't necessarily provide the best advice, and good advice can come from someone ranked lower in the company. When we turn to God for answers, it is amazing to see how things begin to fall into place. He speaks so loud and clear, yet His voice is drowned out by our pride telling us we are capable of handling any situation alone.

Saul fell into this trap while preparing for battle against the Philistines. God provided very specific instructions to wait for Samuel before preparing the burnt offerings as a sacrifice. Saul grew impatient and fearful as he waited for Samuel's arrival. When Saul observed his troops were beginning to slip away, he went ahead without Samuel and offered the sacrifices to God. When Samuel finally arrived, he couldn't believe what Saul had done. Saul's impatience led to an impulsive decision, and his disobedience resulted in the loss of his dynasty.

Impatience is a common characteristic in all of us. We want answers now, and if they're not provided immediately, we make impulsive decisions, which often result in error and misjudgment. God's call for us to serve takes patience and perseverance. His timing is always perfect, although it may not make sense to us. Just when things are going smoothly is often when we hear His compelling call, asking us to leave our comfort zone to serve His purpose.

An associate of mine worked with a company whose office environment was very difficult to handle at times. Managers could be very demeaning in their style, often demoralizing to those who were beneath them. They never sought the advice from their teams because they felt their best advice was their own. I asked my associate why he still worked there when he could go elsewhere and be much happier. His response was that his mission was God's purpose. He knew his boss had little faith and although she called herself a Christian, her actions often went against her beliefs. My associate felt he was called to represent Christ in her life by being a positive and diligent worker, despite the conditions he faced every day.

When faith becomes our most important priority, we can't help but want to serve because that's exactly what Christ calls us to do. Praying to God for advice is a means of serving Him. When we turn to our faith for guidance, a servant role becomes the most desired role. Yet for many in the corporate world, praying is never an option in the decision-making process. We keep our faith outside the office walls, which ultimately means we keep God outside of our corporate lives. Although we believe God can help with our personal matters, how could He possibly run a company better than us?

We can't even conceive faith playing any role in our business, yet we allow business to play a significant role in our lives. Serving begins the moment we turn away from pride and turn toward our faith for guidance on every matter both personally and professionally. When we accept our roles as a God-given position to serve, we realize how limited we are in our abilities and know that without God, we risk everything.

However, we have deadlines to meet and we seek the quick fix. We take matters into our own hands, simply because waiting on God's answer may not meet our deadline. It is important to remember that prayers are always heard and answered in God's time, not ours. And when we listen with our hearts, His answer is often right in front of us.

"Fools think they need no advice, but the wise listen to others."

PROVERBS 12:15).

When decisions have to be made that affect others on our team, there is no better place to turn than God to guide us down the right path. So often I found myself relying solely on the advice of those with bigger titles, knowing in my heart that their advice was not in the best interest of my team.

I fell into this trap when things were not going well at work and we started feeling a little desperate about hitting our revenue projections. We were just coming off a successful holiday season, and many of our clients spent less in the first months of the year since most of their inventory was on sale and they were managing new products arriving for spring.

I had been in this business long enough to know the seasonal pattern of advertising expenditures, yet there was a time where I allowed my boss to force a decision down my throat, knowing in my heart it was a bad move.

We still had budgets to make in January and February, and my boss decided to introduce a "fire sale" to advertisers, encouraging them to spend money during those months. The concept was brilliant, but the way the package was designed was ineffective. Many of the commercials were scheduled to run during lower listening times on the radio. It was the wrong package to present, and although I expressed concerns, he refused to listen. We ended up launching the program.

Needless to say, we received a good response. In the short term, we generated new revenue that was completely unexpected. However, I still had uneasiness about this decision, knowing that the schedule would provide minimal results for our clients.

Unfortunately, my concerns were valid. After the advertising ran, we heard many complaints from our clients that the results were nominal. We had jeopardized our credibility by placing our budgetary needs first over serving our customers, in order to bring short-term success to our company.

In my heart, I knew I should have paid attention to my conscience. Perhaps God was warning me. He has a way of placing heaviness on our conscience, alerting us to be careful. It is His subtle way of providing help— His way of instinctively showing us right from wrong. We choose to either listen to our conscience or ignore it. In this case, I ignored it and chose to focus on my short-term results, ignoring any long-term repercussions. Seeking advice from others is critical, but praying is additionally essential. Had I taken the time to listen to my heart cautioning me, the end result would have been different.

Praying reminds us that our lives are in His control. And looking at our position from a servant perspective is simply reflecting what Christ did for us.

When we choose the advice of others exclusively instead of seeking God's help, we run the risk of making wrong choices. For example, how often do we experience the pressure of hiring someone just to fill a position? What about the time we made a sale, knowing in our heart that it wasn't in the client's best interest—but it got our bosses off our backs?

We simply get caught up in getting the job done, which often becomes a disservice to others. When we place the needs of others above our own, it keeps us from making rash decisions and helps us look at matters from every perspective and not just our own.

I once asked a business associate what she believed was the most important element behind her success. The response was simply, "I have a clear conscious. I sleep well at night."

How many of us can truthfully say the same thing? This associate prayed about every matter in her life, especially ones that related to business. She slept well at night knowing that God's presence was with her. And she knew that in the decisions she faced both personally and professionally, He would guide her down the right path. She was a servant of her faith and thus became a servant in her life.

Praying is an essential component of serving. It's not to say that praying will provide answers quickly, but when we take the time to evaluate our situation, welcoming God's hand in the process, the outcome will produce results where everyone benefits. It may not appear at first to be the best business decision, but it will be the right decision from a divine perspective.

God always expects us to do what's right, and when we take on a servant role, doing what is right becomes bottom line. God opens our eyes to both short-term and long-term thinking as we place our needs in line behind His purpose for us.

Often we pray for things when truthfully we already know what we should do. I knew I should have stood firmer with my boss and redesigned the advertising package so it would serve both our clients' needs *and* the company's needs. I knew that was the right thing to do, but I allowed my title to decide the outcome, managing the situation without any input from those who knew the clients better than I did.

We don't serve God by praying for things He already expects from us. God instructs us to do what is right, so we shouldn't pray for something to become right when we know in our heart that it's wrong. At this point, our focus shouldn't be on praying, but on obeying.

Serving requires us to reach out to God on all matters. Listen to your heart and pray fervently, seeking His wisdom, even if it means allowing for additional time to make the best possible decision. The Lord will never mislead you, but will only offer direction and invaluable insight through sincere and honest prayer.

Once we seek His advice, we need to be prepared to serve where He wants us to be. It won't always be the easy path. In fact, it may appear to be the most difficult way. We will come up with hundreds of excuses why we can't go, but rest assured, if God has called you to serve, the path He has prepared will have successful results.

Moses is a perfect example of a man who was apparently content managing his life as a shepherd. But then one day, God called him to serve way outside his comfort zone.

He led a very simple life as he herded sheep, and most likely Moses was very satisfied and content. He wasn't campaigning for a limelight position, and by society's standards he wasn't even suited to be a leader. But God sees our qualities differently than we do, and uses them to help serve His purpose over our own.

One day when Moses was tending his sheep, God revealed Himself. By the world's standards, others would have been a more suitable leader than Moses, but God saw things differently. What we think is logical may be illogical from a divine perspective. God appointed Moses as "president." In that role, he would serve God's people by leading them out of Egypt.

Out of fear and uncertainty, Moses came up with many excuses why he wasn't prepared to serve God:

"I'm not a good speaker."

"No one will believe me."

"I'm not capable of this."

What excuses do we come up with when we decide managing is better than serving?

"I don't need God's advice."

"I prefer taking matters into my own hands."

"I was promoted; therefore, I have the knowledge to lead."

"It's too difficult to serve God."

There are hundreds of excuses we will use to avoid taking a servant role, but the main one will be our ego telling us we are above serving others. However, here is an important reality to consider: One day, you will lose your job and be replaced by someone else. Remember, in the corporate world everyone is replaceable. One day, something bad will happen in your life. This is the world in which we live. How you handle that "one day" will depend on where God is in your life.

When we live with little faith, we live with little potential. We settle for the simple tasks in life, performing the duties required of us, confining our abilities to the job and title on our business card. We can simply look at where we are today with a limited perspective and be content with the course we have chosen.

Moses most likely would have preferred keeping his life limited to caring for sheep. However, something happened in his heart that changed the course of his life forever: Faith

Faith erased all of Moses excuses to serve. We must erase our excuses as well. When we choose to serve, God takes us beyond our limitations. Was it easy for Moses to lead the people out of Egypt? Were there obstacles along the way? For Moses, it must have been the most difficult challenge of his life. But when we choose to serve, it becomes the most rewarding experience we will ever have.

Failure becomes apparent when we choose to manage our affairs without faith. We are not meant to live in mediocrity, but to live with a divine purpose. Serving provides purpose. In God's eyes, we are irreplaceable. We are not forgotten and we were given the gifts of our abilities to invest beyond our own interests. The abilities that God has instilled go beyond the boundaries of reading reports, analyzing data and responding to e-mails. Integrity lives in a servant's heart, and faith teaches us how to acquire this standard of living.

Serving also applies to our personal lives at home. Many of us have been given the gift of parenthood. We are called not only to discipline our children, but also to serve them for God's purpose. We serve our families by doing what God expects of us. We are expected to serve by supporting and providing, and we are expected to serve by living as His example. We serve by giving our valuable time to our children, simply by reading them a book at night or cleaning the house unexpectedly.

Serving involves doing the expected, but most importantly it requires doing the unexpected. Serving is thanking someone out of the blue. Serving is having coffee with a subordinate and asking him to share his ideas about how the team could do things better. Serving is donating time or money and not telling anyone about it.

Those with a strong faith find serving a natural part of their day. Those who serve are ones who spend more time asking questions than providing advice. Serving requires us to listen intently because often God uses others to tell us what we need to know, even if it's what we don't want to hear.

My son once told me about a situation where his best friend was being critical and making fun of him. I asked him how he handled the situation, expecting to hear that he shot back with a verbal rebuttal that resulted in an argument. To my surprise, this was not the case at all. He simply walked away. Serving his friendship was more important than determining who would win the argument.

As parents, we are so quick to give our kids advice on how to handle every situation because we feel our experience and age make us more intelligent on life's matters. In this example, keeping my mouth shut—instead of giving him advice about managing the situation—was serving my son. He did exactly what Christ would have done. Jesus didn't start an argument with those who rejected His message. He simply spoke the truth to all who would listen and walked away from those who didn't. He even served by doing the unexpected and prayed for His enemies.

God uses people to show us how to become a servant. When we look at our positions from God's perspective, our task of serving takes on an entirely new meaning. One who serves seeks God's invaluable insight and also listens to the advice of others. Serving means understanding we are only as good at the people who work with us. Serving means using our titles to help others succeed, and create an environment for both the company and its employees to win. However, serving is not solely for leaders. It is for everyone within an organization. God's purpose for you in your position may be different than what you have on your personal agenda. However, despite the title you wear, God places us in positions for His mission, which always leads us down the right path.

Have you ever worked for someone who is impossible to work for? Their demands exceed realistic expectations, and their manipulative style is a means of obtaining personal gain.

Perhaps our role as servants is to soften the hearts of those we work with who do not know God. At any level, as persons within an organization, we are to be His example, which will be far more personally gratifying than any title or paycheck. This will require us to submit to our bosses and acknowledge their position of authority. It will mean holding our tongues and remaining positive in our attitudes despite adverse situations.

Paul even spoke about this in his letter to Titus. This doesn't mean that we participate in wrongful actions. However, there will be many instances when we won't always agree with the actions of our superiors. Being negative only fuels the problem and the end result will always lead to destruction. We can either choose to serve God's purpose in our jobs, or strictly manage on our own.

How frustrating it must have been for Moses to see time and time again the people of Israel turning away from their faith. Their demands became excessive, and despite all of the miracles God provided, the people were skeptical and negative. However, Moses was reminded that his purpose as a leader was not his own, but God's. Moses was simply an instrument God was using to save His people.

Perceiving our roles as servants in both our jobs and at home allows for God's purpose to prevail. When we refrain from being negative and listening to our prideful hearts, we reflect His work in our lives and demonstrate the place we have given Him.

A job can have either God's purpose in mind, or our own. We can choose to be Saul or Moses simply by making the decision to serve or to manage.

> *"Don't be selfish; don't live to make a good impression on others. Be humble, thinking of others as better than yourself. Don't think only about your own affairs, but be interested in others, too, and what they are doing.*

> *Your attitude should be the same that Christ Jesus had. Though he was God, he did not demand and cling to his rights as God. He made himself nothing; he took the humble position of a slave and appeared in human form. And in human form he obediently humbled himself even further by dying a criminal's death on a cross"*

PHILIPPIANS 2:3–8

chapter Eleven

RUN FROM TEMPTATION

"So why do you call me 'Lord,' when you won't obey me?
I will show you what it's like when someone comes to me, listens
to my teaching, and then obeys me.
It is like a person who builds a house on a strong foundation
laid upon the underlying rock.
When the floodwaters rise and break against the house, it
stands firm because it is well built.
But anyone who listens and doesn't obey is like a person who
builds a house without a foundation. When the flood sweep down
against that house, it will crumble into a heap of ruins."

LUKE 6:46–49

When we hear the word "temptation," the first biblical image that comes to mind is the story of Adam and Eve in the Book of Genesis. The Lord had said they could eat any of the fruit, except that from the tree of the knowledge of good and evil.

The serpent, the shrewdest of all created things, convinced Eve to eat the fruit from that tree, even though the Lord specifically warned against it. Eve was tempted to do what she knew in her heart was wrong.

There are many stories in the Bible that deal with temptation. We will always be faced with temptation in both our personal and professional world. Temptation is the act of evil desires that pull us away from God by feeding on our areas of weakness. It is the voice that says to us, "No one will know," "No one will be harmed," "You need this."

Why do we allow ourselves to be tempted, even when we know temptation is the basis for our wrongful actions? What do we gain from it? Is what we gain greater than the integrity we lose?

In the corporate world, temptation comes in all shapes and sizes. Greed is often the form it takes. The more at stake, the more we become tempted. Often, managers conduct business that goes against corporate policy as though nothing were wrong so they can gain financially from their actions. Others follow along, often knowing it's wrong, perhaps because they fear that if they speak up, they could lose their jobs.

I had a dream one night that caused me to wake up in a state of fear. My dream was that Satan had given me a locked box. Despite knowing in my heart that the contents were harmful, I tried to open it. There were two keys. The first one didn't work, but I didn't stop there. I quickly grabbed the second key, which unlocked the box. Once it was opened, I realized I had done something horrible. As I stepped away from the box, there was a huge explosion. I woke up immediately, frightened by how easily I had been tempted. I knew my actions were wrong, but I was tempted by curiosity about what could possibly be in the box.

We are all subjected to different types of temptation, and we fall easily into its trap. We're given boxes every day that we know we shouldn't open. We ignore the voice of our subconscious and are willing to sacrifice our integrity just to see what's inside.

As leaders of our organizations, we must resist opening the box of temptation. In fact, run from it. God has selected you to be in this position of leadership for a reason. What message as leaders do we send when our actions indicate we've caved in to temptation?

Greed, vanity and power are three common motivators behind temptation. We convince ourselves that we've earned our way, and therefore the perks that come along tempt us. We accept jobs that pay higher salaries, knowing that it will demand more of our time away from our families. Titles build greed and vanity. We may receive more stuff, but is it really worth the sacrifice of time away from our families and faith?

"And yet you say, 'I haven't done anything wrong. Surely he isn't angry with me!' Now I will punish you severely because you claim you have not sinned"

JEREMIAH 2:35

Individuals who fall to temptation will eventually fall to their demise. We preach to our employees about the corporate policies, but we make exceptions for those with more clout. We sacrifice our character and integrity. We are all guilty of this, whether we want to admit it or not.

Greed became my temptation by accepting a job, sacrificing time away from my family, in order to make more money. My desire to make more money became more important than the value of the time I could spend with my family. We didn't need the extra income, but greed has a way of convincing us that we can't live without certain materialist things. We obsess to possess the things that we feel will make our lives more satisfying, only to find out that once we obtain something, we only want something more.

Looking back on all of those years, there is no amount of money that can buy back the time I lost to be with the people I love most. Greed fed temptation, placing everything else, including my faith and family, second in my life. Time is our most valuable asset, and yet it is one of God's gifts that we often sacrifice to fulfill our personal desires and needs.

The corporate world exposes us to all types of temptation. We abuse our titles and positions by falling to temptation so that we receive some level of personal gain. Usually, power and authority are gained at the expense of integrity. There is no price to gauge the value of integrity, but once we fall to temptation, we lose what God values so much in our hearts. Don't believe for a minute that our actions go unnoticed by God. What we consider a tiny blemish will receive enormous repercussions. Consider yourself in a dangerous position when you're willing to sacrifice your integrity.

Solomon, one of the greatest kings that ever lived, fell into temptation. The Bible shares Solomon's greatest moments as king, and his most tragic downfalls. In the beginning, Solomon promised God he would live according to God's laws. Through the blessings of God, he was given more money, power and authority than any other king.

> *"Then the LORD appeared to Solomon a second time, as he had done before at Gibeon. The LORD said to him, 'I have heard your prayer and your request. I have set apart this Temple you have built so that my name will be honored there forever. I will always watch over it and care for it. As for you, if you will follow me with integrity and godliness, as David your father did, always obeying my commands and keeping my laws and regulations, then I will establish the throne of your dynasty over Israel forever. For I made this promise to your father, David: 'You will never fail to have a successor on the throne of Israel.'"*

1 KINGS 9:2–5

However, Solomon couldn't keep his part—the "if" part—of the promise. His downfall occurred when his actions went against what God had instructed. God ruled against intermarriage with the nations around Israel and Solomon fell to temptation by marrying multiple wives from other nations. He began to worship other gods that his wives introduced him to, turning further away from the Lord. He knew in his heart that what he was doing was wrong, but he did it anyway.

The Book of Ecclesiastes is Solomon's confession where he shares his life experience and warns us that the pleasures of this earth are only temporary.

> *"So I became greater than any of the kings who ruled in Jerusalem before me. And with it all, I remained clear-eyed so that I could evaluate all these things. Anything I wanted, I took. I did not restrain myself from any joy. I even found great pleasure in hard work, an additional reward for all my labors. But as I looked at everything I had worked so hard to accomplish, it was all so meaningless. It was like chasing the wind."*

(ECCLESIASTES 2:9–11

When we turn away from God, we can easily fall to temptation. Diverting our focus from our faith leads us down this path. Temptation feeds on our inadequacies. One of the greatest weaknesses in believing we are strong is that our vulnerabilities become the source of temptation. Often when we are tempted, we don't stop to consider what consequences we may face because our focus is not on God. Instead, we focus on ourselves and our personal desires.

Temptation is very real and can enter our lives at our weakest or even strongest moments. For Solomon, temptation struck when things were going so well. He was at the top of his career, consumed by money, power and authority. Prosperity and success can fill us with pride, placing our needs above God's expectations and hopes for us. This is an easy trap to fall into. When things are going well, we fail to acknowledge God's hand in our successes and temptation slips in.

> *"But that is the time to be careful! Beware that in your plenty you do not forget the LORD your God and disobey his commands, regulations and laws. For when you have become full and prosperous and have built fine homes to live in, and when your flocks and herds have become very large and your silver and gold have multiplied along with everything else, that is the time to be careful."*

DEUTERONOMY 8:11–14

We can choose to give into temptation, or we can run from it. Either way, the choice is ours to make. The stronger our faith, the easier it is to resist. The weaker our faith, the easer it is to fall.

Joseph's faith was strong, showing him how to run from temptation and its evil desires. Joseph could have chosen to commit adultery, but refused to become a victim of temptation. His fear of God and the consequences of his actions were far greater than the desire that temptation created in his life.

At some point, we will be placed in compromising situations that could destroy us if we fell to temptation. Do we live with the same fear of God today as Joseph did? For many of us, the answer is no. We only fear the consequences of getting caught by those around us more than we fear that judgment that waits for us. We believe the repercussions we face on earth are far worse than facing the wrath of God.

Run from temptation. It will never lead you down the right path in life.

Temptation is nothing more than deception, and eventually the consequences will be far greater than any personal reward or desire.

> "God blesses the people who patiently endure testing. Afterward they will receive the crown of life that God has promised to those who love him. And remember, no one who wants to do wrong should ever say, 'God is testing me.' God is never tempted to do wrong, and he never tempts anyone else either. Temptation comes from the lure of our own evil desires. These evil desires lead to evil actions, and evil actions lead to death."

JAMES 1:12–15

chapter Twelve

TURN OFF THE NOISE

*"Those who love to talk will experience the consequences, for
the tongue can kill or nourish life."*

PROVERBS 18:21

In the early 90s, I worked for one of the largest Internet companies. This was a very exciting time in my corporate career. The Internet was changing the way we communicated. Human interaction was taking place through computers and information was being provided at the touch of a keyboard. It was always amazing to visit our corporate offices and hear the silence on each floor, knowing that hundreds of employees were busy at work.

Staff meetings were conducted via desktop computers, and phone conversations were rare. So much of our company's business was done without the sound of human voices. In fact, there were many instances when I never physically saw my boss. We communicated strictly through instant messaging on our desktops. This was considered the norm. Looking back, we must have appeared robotic to the world.

It was fascinating to observe the expressions on people's faces when we told them the Internet would become a primary source of communication between customers and businesses. Most companies thought we were crazy. Many claimed the Internet would never be a means of selling products and services. Customers wanted human interaction, and a computer wasn't going to replace it.

More than ten years have passed since I worked for AOL, and today, more businesses rely on e-mail to communicate with customers and employees than ever before. The question is: How much of our face-to-face interaction has been replaced by e-mail? On an average working day, I often received as many as forty to seventy e-mails a day, each demanding an immediate response. Over 90 percent of my responses were typed and not spoken. In the business world, we need answers quickly, and more often than not, we don't want a phone call. We expect an e-mail response.

After spending hours sifting through my e-mails, I realize that most of them represent nothing more than wasted conversations about matters counterproductive to the business at hand. E-mail has created more chatter in our lives than any other form of communication. At AOL, we referred to the chatter as "the swirl." Swirl represented conversations that stirred matters up but had nothing to do with business. They were simply typed messages filled with gossip and junk.

Swirl is the wasted communication that does nothing to benefit—and sometimes destroys—those around us. We would never have these conversations face-to face, but e-mail today has become a place where boundaries are expanded beyond what used to be considered professionally or politically correct. E-mail can be the noisiest and most distractive form of communication, where a lot is said, but with very little significance.

The phrase "multi-tasking" has taken on a whole new meaning. We conduct multiple conversations with different individuals simultaneously over our desktops. At AOL, I could have twenty instant messages on my screen at any given time. Twenty different people were speaking to me, vying for my attention. Imagine being in a conference room when this many people are talking to you the same time? How much of any conversation would you be able to hear, or—even more importantly—give much thought to in formulating your response?

Why would we need human interaction when computers can conduct all of our conversations? As we continue down the path of becoming more technologically savvy, the need for human interaction is becoming irrelevant in the business world. I must honestly admit that many customers I worked with rarely heard my voice. If we needed to express emotion in an e-mail, we learned how to type smiley faces or sad faces. We even had expressions for confusion, frustration and boredom.

Managers often use capital letters as a means of yelling at their employees. It became OK to use harsh words in an e-mail, but if the words were said in person, it would have been considered unacceptable.

Today, we are interacting more, yet saying less. Technology has substantially increased the noise in our lives, adding more distractions and disruptive communication, making it more difficult to hear those messages that could truly impact our personal and professional world.

How much noise do we have in our lives today and, most importantly, how much of it do we personally create? The noise I am referring to is not the technology itself, but the messages within it. The messages we send to others come in all shapes and sizes, and depending on how the information is presented, these communications can be the most counterproductive and destructive means of getting the attention of others.

Swirl is nothing more than gossip and destructive information that as a society we thrive on in our daily communications. We are enamored with the lives of others, more than we are enamored with the life we are given. Technology makes communication appear less destructive because it comes from a computer, but its impact can have even greater adverse results.

Technology supposedly offers a means of simplifying our lives, allowing for more time to do things that are personally important to us. Many aspects of technology have made things easier, yet the challenge becomes the amount of time we spend in front of computers, PDAs and television sets.

The truth is that technology has made us busier today than ever before by creating additional noise. We may think we are more productive, but the question becomes: Are we more effective? Technology makes us accessible to our jobs twenty-four hours a day, beyond the required forty-hour week in our offices. We check our e-mails after our kids go to bed, and many of us can't shut off our PDAs after 5 P.M.

I remember walking into my office at 7:30 A.M. and having my boss ask if I had had a chance to read the e-mail he had sent the prior evening. He wasn't able to shut the noise off, and he expected us to suffer from the same disorder. Today, technology may simplify communication to some extent, but more often than not, we have allowed it to drain more of our time, leaving us less time for everything else.

The Internet has changed the way we do business and the way we communicate in our lives. However, the challenge we face is being able to shut it down not only from a time perspective but also to keep it from replacing human interaction in our lives.

E-mail should never be a means of replacing a voice. If we have become so busy that our time is too important for personal meetings, then we are doing a disservice to our companies, families and our faith.

Genuine communication will never exist through technology because technology is only a representation of the face-to-face interaction of human beings who make the time to be in contact with one another. Genuine communication allows us to read between the lines and listen beyond the words being spoken. A personal meeting will uncover more information than any e-mail possibly can. Thirty years ago, much of the sales training in use dealt with non-verbal communication. This includes facial expressions, eye contact and hand gestures that reveal one's true message behind what they verbalize. Today, there is far less attention given to this type of communication than ever before.

We even experience this at home. As parents, many of us consider text messaging an acceptable means of communication. We say it is better to communicate with our teen this way than have no communication at all. This is a valid statement, but at what point did we determine that technology should replace our personal contact with our children?

A computer will never be able to provide genuine communication. It cannot read between the lines, and it cannot reflect one's feelings that come only from the heart. It may be one's only means of communication, but we cannot depend on it to be genuine. We are not capable of reading each other's minds. Therefore, if e-mail has become the primary source of communication, it's important to note that technology is made up of noise, and not the heart.

Technology is one of the biggest factors in the noise in our lives. The increased use of computers, television and PDAs creates more distractions and drains even more of our time for other pursuits. When we live in the noise, the noise becomes a part of us. We, as parents, set the example of how much noise we allow into our homes.

We are role models for our children. Our kids will reflect what we model as an acceptable amount of time we allow for the noise. We use the noise to drown out the voices of our kid—or our spouses. We blame the noise for the time we choose to take reading our e-mails. We are passive to the noise during the hours we spend in front of our television sets. The noise keeps things at a distance and impersonal. It becomes a place to hide so we don't have to reveal true emotions.

The business world is less personal today because of the increased noise that has entered the walls of our offices. Less human interaction and more disruptive communication live in both our business and personal lives. We have become so dependent on it that the noise has become a part of us.

I remember sometimes feeling guilty when I asked for a vacation day. I just wanted one day to regroup and spend with my family, but I could never fully enjoy the moment because work remained in the back of my mind. E-mail was at the tip of my fingers. The events of my work life often remained spinning in the back of my mind.

For many, taking time off can actually be more stressful than going to work. Winding down was a challenge in my life, and the guilt of not being in the office could be consuming. It is amazing that we even allow this guilt to ever exist.

We punish ourselves for relaxing. We fill our silence for fear of missing the latest news story. We don't allow for quiet and still moments, even for a minute to spend with God.

I used to have more than a one-hour drive into work every morning, and for some reason, the radio had to be on for background noise. I was never actually listening to it, but I preferred the sound of noise to silence. I was incapable of turning off the noise. My ambition to live in the noise was far greater than any desire to live a quiet and peaceful life guided by faith.

The noise in our lives goes beyond what comes out of our mouths or what we listen to. It is also part of how we utilize our time. We live in a fast-paced world. The activities in our lives require endless hours of hard work, time and dedication. We wake up every morning and leave for our offices before the light of the sun has filled the sky. We fill our days with meetings and busy schedules.

We fill the lives of our children with activities and events so they too lead a hectic life. We think that if we keep them busy enough with enough toys and programs, we won't hear their complaint, "I'm bored." But in the process we rob them of their own creative quiet and reflective moments and the sheer joy of being a kid.

We allow ourselves to burn the candle at both ends (sometimes dragging our children into it as well), knowing that burnout is going to be the end result. Before we know it, the day is over and we ask ourselves: *Where did the day go?* Hopefully, we catch ourselves before we have to ask the question: *Where did my life go?*

At what point do we finally take a moment and turn off the noise? Is it truly guilt that stirs up the noise in our lives that makes us feel we must work those extra few hours on Saturday just to stay ahead? Or is it simply our ambition taken to such a degree that we'll do anything to make it happen, even if it means increasing the noise in our lives? Perhaps we stay busy for the sake of keeping busy, blaming the noise on the demands that we've placed on ourselves, and overlooking what God's purpose may be in our lives.

Technology has made us less personal and will increase the level of noise in our lives as we allow more of it to come in. It's the swirl behind the technology that is even more damaging than the technology itself. We spend countless hours engaged in destructive conversations centered on the lives of others with our IMing, texting and e-mailing. All of these allow for demoralizing conversations simply because we are not confronting our victims face-to-face. It's time to shut it down and turn off the noise.

*"And why worry about a speck in your friend's eye when you have a log
in your own?"*

MATTHEW 7:3

The tongue is not intended to defame others, but it is to be used as a
tool for serving and providing words of encouragement. We spend more
time today consumed in our own chatter than we do listening with our
hearts. There is nothing more satisfying than a person who listens to every
word you're saying while keeping their mouth shut. Often the best advice
is no advice at all when someone wants us to simply listen with our hearts,
an act that is one of God's greatest gifts but something we so underutilize
in our lives. We all know the talkers in our lives. We don't have enough
fingers to count all of them. How many of us know of at least one good listener?

In 1985, I was an account executive for a radio station. We were
responsible for selling commercial time. The title of the gentleman who ran
our station was General Manager. He had multiple individuals reporting to
him as well as his other corporate responsibilities.

E-mail was nonexistent at that time. All communication between
employees and customers was done in person or over the phone. Each
week, my GM would have lunch with either an employee or customer of
our radio station. This was the time he dedicated to getting to know others
within the company and our customers. Except for the questions he asked,
he rarely spoke during our conversations. He also used this time to hear
from our customers and learn about their businesses.

There were often times when we had lunch with customers who were
unhappy. Our General Manager never spent the time defending our business practices, but listened instead for possible opportunities for improve-
ment. Needless to say, he became very well known and loved by his staff
and the business community. It was not only the time that he took to be
with people, but also the level of conversation that transpired. He truly
wanted to know the people reporting to him. He asked questions about our
personal lives, ambitions and goals. This General Manager may have been
the extreme of being an effective listener, but working for him was a true

inspiration. He truly felt he had more to learn from others than what he could teach us. This was all done through listening, instead of talking. We were very dedicated to his success as he was to ours.

Often we are the ones who create the noise. We are quick to defend our position whether we are in the right or the wrong. What we believe to be communicating is actually nothing more than noise for others to hear. The message goes in one ear and out the other.

Good listeners are diligent individuals who embrace a quiet and gentle spirit. They are usually the last to speak and the first to communicate. It is interesting to see an effective listener in a meeting. They hang on every word spoken and are intuitive observers. They are able to hear beyond what is being said, listening for possible motives behind the actual words being spoken. Their line of questioning probes deeper than the expected. They look for information that comes not from the mouth, but from the heart. They are also the ones who never respond to massive e-mails that circulate in the office that request opinions on matters of potential conflict. They are quick to identify the noise within the message, especially from e-mails that carry a particular tone. We now use e-mail as a means to shout at others simply by capitalizing every word typed. Often managers demand quick responses to their problems. Listeners never respond by e-mail, but rather approach the matter face-to-face.

How does one turn off the noise and become a good listener? Is it simply the act of keeping one's mouth shut? For me, I always believed this was the case, but through many experiences of my life, I have determined keeping quiet is only the first step.

On Sunday mornings at church, we are "forced" to listen to the sermon that is given. We sit there quietly, hoping to hear our minister share what we hope will be a profound message. We want to be inspired by his or her words, trusting they will motivate us to do what is right. For many of us, this may be the only time we actually listen attentively, and more importantly, care about what is being said.

What is it about God's Word that speaks to many of us directly? How often do we hear a sermon that shows us the reality in our hearts? I never knew how to really listen until I began studying Scripture.

God has a way of speaking to us through words that painfully point out the examples of when we were talking when we should have been listening. He also reveals those moments when we should have spoken, and we chose to remain silent.

God's advice provides a very powerful message that resonates above the noise in our lives and speaks to our hearts. I have learned firsthand how much the truth can hurt, and from that experience I have learned to listen beyond the words being spoken and uncover one's feelings that live in their heart. There is a wonderful sound behind silencing our own voices. For many, the silence is what makes everything uncomfortable.

We were taught in many sales training courses that the first one who speaks is the one who loses. Personally, I never understood what that meant, but followed its advice only to find myself staring at the other individual who was also trained the same way.

At one time, silence was uncomfortable for me. I always felt someone should be talking or there should be background noise playing. Yet, it is the element of silence that calms our spirit. Silence has the power to relieve our stress; however, many of us find silence to be stressful. Silence is one of our greatest assets, yet it is so often underutilized. We have become so accustomed to having noise and distraction in our lives that when we do find moments of silence, we become uncomfortable. Church forces us to turn off the noise, even for just an hour. While we sit quietly waiting to hear our minister's message, this becomes God's moment. Shutting out the noise becomes God's opportunity to speak to our hearts. The message isn't always positive, and can often touch a nerve, but we hear it and even for the slightest moment, it has the power to impact our lives.

"And as Elijah stood there, the LORD passed by, and a mighty windstorm hit the mountain. It was such a terrible blast that the rocks were torn loose, but the LORD was not in the wind. After the wind, there was an earthquake, but the LORD was not in the earthquake. And after the earthquake, there was a fire, but the LORD was not in the fire. And after the fire, there was the sound of a gentle whisper."

1 KINGS 19:11–12

God graciously gives us time on this earth outside of church to listen away from the noise; however, our lives have become too busy to enjoy the moments of silence and hear His voice. We always make time to speak with our bosses. We seem to have excess time to chat with our neighbors, but how often do we talk with God, and listen with our hearts?

This is not to say that God doesn't speak to us above the noise in our lives, but it is most usually in the moments of quietness that we become moved by His message. Sunday's sermon speaks to our hearts, but by Wednesday we have turned up the noise and forgotten what was said. Imagine if that Sunday feeling remained with us the entire week. When we enter our offices, feeling the stress of the day weighing on our shoulders before we even start work, we receive an e-mail with an inspiring message. Or we have an encounter with a coworker who smiles at us when we pass by her desk. The stuff we take for granted may be what He uses to bring us closer to Him. God is compelled by His compassion to reach our hearts, no matter how loud the noise becomes in our lives.

When we get home from our hectic days, God uncovers those tiny moments to get our attention. Just when we've settled ourselves in front of the TV to listen to the noise of our world, a little voice appears from around the corner: "Daddy, do you want to shoot some hoops?" "Mommy, can you help me with my homework?" "Will you watch a movie with me?"

God sometimes uses the voice of our children to shut off the noise. Our children don't care how tired we are or how bad our day was. The only thing that matters to them is our time at home with them. The little voice that we hear may be God's way of asking us to turn off the noise. He will try every angle He can to reach our hearts, but often we are caught up in the distractions that we can't hear Him. How many times do we jump at the requests of our bosses but ignore studying the Bible? We've accumulated endless excuses for not having time for God. Truthfully, we never intended to give Him the time in the first place. The noise in our life is nothing than an excuse to keep God at a distance.

We will chase job after job, title after title, but without reading Scripture and listening to His advice, we will never find contentment. We will pour all of our energy into making more money, only to find that defining ourselves through worldly possessions will leave us empty-handed. Instead of turning to God, the noise turns us in the opposite direction. Perhaps we have prayed for His wisdom but didn't hear a response. Rest assured God has responded—or will respond—but only when we quell the noise, and most importantly, willingly obey.

"If you need wisdom—if you want to know what God wants you to do— ask him, and he will gladly tell you. He will not resent your asking. But when you ask him, be sure that you really expect him to answer, for a doubtful mind is as unsettled as a wave of the sea that is driven and tossed by the wind."

JAMES 1:5–6

When God speaks, often He may say something we don't want to hear. We allow the noise to intercept the message He has provided. However, that little pang of guilt that weighs on our conscience is a reminder that our problems aren't going to be solved by turning up the noise and ignoring His advice.

When we hear the name Jonah, what comes to mind is a story of a prophet who spent some time inside a fish. For many of us, this may be all that we've heard about this man. Jonah ended up inside a fish as a result of his unwillingness to listen to God's instructions. The story of Jonah found in the Bible illustrates that by ignoring God's advice, our lives will be subjected to turmoil, which leads us down the road of uncertainty.

God specifically told Jonah to go to the city of Nineveh where the people had become corrupt. Jonah, who was reluctant to go, turned up the noise and actually went in the opposite direction. He was trying to escape God's request and bought a ticket, got on a ship, hoping he could sail far away from God. A huge storm took over the seas and the crew feared for their lives. Jonah was thrown overboard and upon hitting the water, the storm ceased. He spent the next three days inside a fish.

Fortunately, we can say that none of us have ended up inside a fish because we ran from God's advice, although sitting inside a fish certainly is one way to shut off the noise. When we turn up the noise in our lives as a means of drowning out God's voice, we become unwilling to serve in the way to which He has called us. We are commanded to give time to our faith. We are called to learn the Bible. We are called to live as an example of Christ. How many years must we allow to pass before we acknowledge His presence and purpose for our lives? The more noise we allow, the greater distance we create between God and His purpose for us.

> *"Today you must listen to his voice.*
> *Don't harden your hearts against him."*

HEBREWS 4:7

I sat through a sermon at church one Sunday listening to our minister talk about a Bible study that required a huge time commitment, but he said the return on our investment of time would change our lives. This particular class required hours of reading and studying Scripture. As I listened to our minister speak about the importance of Bible studies, I thought to myself that if I could ever find the time, I would take that particular course. I knew in my heart studying Scripture was something I should do, but I never allowed the time. My day was filled with other responsibilities, and the noise seemed to be more important than obtaining a deeper understanding of my faith. I actually said to myself, *God, if you can find time in my busy life, I will take this class.*

God heard my request, and a few weeks later, I was informed my company was closing their offices and I could choose to leave, or move to New York. I suppose the moral of the story is to be careful what you pray for! Suddenly, I had a lot of time on my hands because moving to New York was not an option. Despite the anxiety I felt over not having a job, I decided to keep my promise and signed up for the Bible class.

Studying Scripture is one of the most effective ways to turn off the noise in our lives. The Bible provides timeless information and is a vehicle God uses to speak to our hearts. His message is not always flowery, but certainly rewarding. We find ourselves relating to the same challenges today that existed over 2,000 years ago.

Studying Scripture forces us to look deep into our hearts, defining our true priorities and determining what part our faith plays in our lives. The virtue of humility enhances our ability to listen. One must have a humble spirit to be able to listen beyond the words spoken. For me, God used Scripture to point out holes in my character. It never occurred to me that all I had accomplished were gifts from Him, and seeing for the first time how He was using me to help serve His purpose. God never hesitates to hear our prayers, but when we pray for advice, He expects us to listen, and more importantly, to obey what we hear.

I had used every excuse in the past for not having enough time for my faith. These excuses were nothing more than the noise in my life. Our lives will always be busy. The real question is whether the noise comes before faith, or faith before the noise.

God shows us how to turn off the noise and enjoy the silence that brings us closer to Him. God expects us to work hard and lead a quiet life. This means ending the gossiping and chatter. This will require us to shut down the disruptive communication conveyed in our e-mails. This means coming home and spending time with our family, and most importantly, our faith. God wants us to lift away the barriers that we've built to keep Him at a distance.

Driving in my car without the radio on has become a treat in my day, and although the demands of my life remain constant, a sense of peace and serenity exists that wipes away the anxiety. Does it mean the noise is completely eliminated from my life? No, when we live in the world, we live in the noise we and others create, so we determine how much time we give to it.

I have become more aware of my actions and the purpose He wants me to fulfill. God revealed to me in Scripture how to live contently and satisfied with my life. Most importantly, He showed me how to shut off the noise.

Once we open our hearts and listen for His voice, it's imperative that we obey His instructions. God is happy to provide guidance, but don't ask if you don't plan to obey. He doesn't always tell us what we want to hear, but if we choose to obey, our reward is far greater than following our own instinct.

God instructs the alcoholic that he must change his ways. God tells us as parents who use harsh and demoralizing words that He favors a tender spirit over a prideful heart. The woman who gossips is reminded that her conduct is as repulsive to God as one who murders. God points out our downfalls—not as a punishment tactic, but so we can repent. If we listen, and obey, God will forgive our wayward lives, and show us how to live with fulfillment and purpose.

Jonah spent three days inside a fish, asking for God's forgiveness and advice. He turned off the noise, listened and obeyed. He was no longer afraid to go to Nineveh. When God gives us advice, He never leaves us to handle the matter alone. He remains at our side at all times, giving us the courage and strength to fulfill whatever mission He has in store for us.

I knew in my heart I had to change my ways. Choosing my next job was not going to be based on titles and income, but as a means of serving Him. Once we are willing to turn off the noise, He begins His work in us.

There are no more excuses to be made. Turn off the noise. Shut down the technology. Quit gossiping, and spend a few moments reading Scripture. Reading the Bible and praying for God's guidance gives us insight into matters to make the right decisions. Turning off the noise allows us to experience firsthand His purpose for our lives.

"And so I tell you, keep on asking, and you will be given what you ask for. Keep on looking, and you will find. Keep on knocking, and the door will be opened. For everyone who asks, receives. Everyone who seeks, finds. And the door is opened to everyone who knocks."

LUKE 11:9–10

chapter Thirteen

THE BATTLE BETWEEN CREATION AND CREATOR

"Don't let the excitement of youth cause you to forget your Creator.
Honor him in your youth before you grow old and
no longer enjoy living."

ECCLESIASTES 12:1

Twenty years have gone by in my life as quickly as a wave washes upon a beach. When we leave our homes, we begin a new life. For many, it is a very exciting time. We start careers, get married, have children, buy homes and live the good life.

For others, it may not be so blissful. We come from broken homes. We've lived through torturous times and leaving home was a means of survival. Some of us choose the right path, while others turn to a dark life that leads to one's demise. There is one thing for certain. We make choices in our lives. Some are good and some are bad. Some will lead us to God, while others will take us further away. Whether our lives on the outside appear to be blissful or not, both kinds of lives become lost when we don't actively involve God.

The path we take is determined by our choice between creation, which is man, and Creator, who is God. Man represents all that is sinful in the world, and Christ represents all that is good. None of us wants to believe we are making choices that go against our faith, but if we are not actively pursuing a relationship with God, the choice has already been made.

God is fighting for our hearts and, whether we admit it or not, we hold the weapons that are being used against Him. When we take a closer look at our lives and everything we have accomplished, what has brought us closer to God?

If you have to ponder this question for more than a few minutes, perhaps you need to look at your life differently. Many of us go through our days with a familiar routine. We wake up, have breakfast, get the kids to school, go to work, come home, eat dinner, watch TV, then go to bed. This schedule is a reflection of a familiar routine many in the world follow 365 days a year. At what point in the mundane activities of life, do we see ourselves pursuing a relationship with God? Sad to say, we spend more of our time filling our days to meet the needs of creation than even considering what our Creator wants from us.

Life on this earth without God is nothing more than a routine of errands and responsibilities. We go through the motions of our day fulfilling our roles, yet never once consider that maybe God has kept things quiet in our lives so we might take a moment to seek His purpose. I had a life very similar to the one just mentioned. I was an expert at getting things done in a timely matter and meeting the obligations set before me.

When we live for creation, life becomes nothing more than a busy routine. Creation fills our days with distractions that become nothing more than excuses to give less time to our faith. God wants us to live an abundant life, but when we set our goals on meeting the needs of creation, the abundance He wants to bless us with is replaced with a mere existence. We never once consider that our daily routines may have nothing to do with fulfilling His purpose. Failure to involve God in our daily routine becomes a weapon we use in the battle for our hearts.

Wealth is another weapon. By valuing our prosperity and all that it provides as the meaning and source of happiness in our lives, we make money a weapon used against God. When we choose to live by our own selfish desires in our effort to get ahead—even if it means hurting others along the way—our selfish desires become a weapon.

When we choose to give our time to people of higher socioeconomic status in our effort to obtain personal gain, this is a weapon. When we never seek God's forgiveness, this is a weapon. Anything that is placed before our faith—including those we love— becomes a weapon. Our neglect to pursue a relationship with our Creator is weapon.

We say we love God, but we continue to do bad things. We want to be a good Christian, but our actions seem to fall one step behind our words. In the corporate world, actions are determined by how we can best reach our revenue goals and objectives. Profitability becomes a weapon when it takes precedence over everything else, including doing what is right. We push for record profit earnings, despite the hurdles we create that cause others to suffer.

In our homes, we are no better. The very words we use can be the most destructive weapon we have. We tear out the hearts of those who love us most. We yell more than we praise. We drink more than we pray. We expect more from our children than we provide. We spend more than we give. We listen to creation more than we listen to God.

"Then I observed that most people are motivated to success by their envy of their neighbors. But this, too, is meaningless, like chasing the wind."

ECCLESIASTES 4:4

It is easy to say we love God and that we are good Christians, but in this world, it is greed, power and money that we choose to love more than our faith. Our obsession is not to grow with God, but to grow in all that we possess. It is not to say that God doesn't want us to have nice things and live comfortably, but when our desire to possess becomes greater than our desire for God, it becomes a weapon.

I attended church as a child and learned about the life of Christ. I knew where He was born and I was told how He died. I memorized the Lord's Prayer and was somewhat familiar with several people mentioned in the Bible, including Noah, Moses and the earthly parents of Jesus, Mary and Joseph. This was the extent of my Bible knowledge. Sad to say, this is the extent of most people's biblical knowledge in their entire lifetime. Choosing not to read the Bible becomes a weapon against our faith.

My life was not about living and learning from my Creator. My life was about living for me, obtaining all that I could, and anything that was left over was given to my faith. My source for truth was not God's Word but the daily newspaper delivered to my home.

We all want nice things and to live the perfect life. However, our perception of a perfect life may be much different than what our faith tells us. Many feel perfection is achieved by what we possess—the more we have, the more perfect life we live. Outward appearances become our obsession. We live to work and work to live, finding no balance for anything else. We believe money will solve all of our problems, only to learn that money actually becomes the problem. Our true interests lie in gaining more prosperity and living beyond the necessary means.

Our jobs can become one of our most destructive weapons we use against our Creator, especially when work becomes an obsession. In the corporate world, we love to hire work alcoholics. It's one of those secret-hiring criteria that we subtly look for in an individual. Résumés filled with countless hours given to jobs and careers are priceless in the working world. If we see too much in the area of outside activities and interests, we may conclude that candidate is lazy or at least, unfocused.

Most companies would say there is nothing wrong with this mindset in the selection process because in today's corporate culture, the time demanded from employees is necessary if they want to succeed. As bosses, we used to say: "If you can't stand the heat, get out of the kitchen."

As interviewees, we are trained to talk little about what we love to do in our free time. In a thirty-minute interview, that question is usually asked last, and is more often than not an afterthought. Corporate America wants all of you and isn't really interested in what you do in the few hours of free time they give you.

Our time is a weapon we use against our faith. We take for granted that tomorrow will come, meetings will be conducted, errands will be run, and our children will be home to greet us after a long day at the office. Creation tells us to rely not on faith, but on our daily calendars, ensuring that we get everything done in a timely manner. A common interview question we asked potential candidates is: "Where do you want to be in five years?"

We are planners. We schedule meetings months out. We plan celebrations years from today. We casually say to our neighbors, "See you next week." Planning is essential in our busy lives, but often what we plan may be different from God's plan for us.

"How do you know what will happen tomorrow? For your life is like the morning fog—it's here a little while, then it's gone. What you ought to say is, 'If the Lord wants us to, we will live and do this or that. Otherwise you will be boasting about your own plans, and all such boasting is evil."

JAMES 4:14–16

Creation is fighting for our time, yet only God knows how much we have left. Time becomes a powerful weapon that creation uses to pull our attention away from our faith. It creates the fallacy in our thinking that we have all the time in the world to get things done. We create visions of what our lives will be like in ten years, overlooking what God's vision of our life is for today. Time on this earth is priceless, and often taken for granted. There is nothing wrong with having visions or hopes for the future—but only if we approach the future as God's will and not our own.

God is fighting for our time. Both creation and Creator demand our full attention and each pulls us in opposite directions to achieve its purpose. In the corporate world, I spent countless hours traveling from city to city, away from my husband and young children. I justified my actions as helping to financially support our needs.

However, I learned over time that my level of financial support was not a necessity, but was prompted instead by a desire to live at a certain level. It wasn't the additional money that we needed, but because I lacked self-confidence, the larger the title, the more confident I became.

I desired approval from presidents and CEOs more than approval from my faith. Therefore, I gave more of my time to creation than to God. My desire to grow in my faith was secondary to growing in my company.

The guilt existed in my heart, but I did nothing to alleviate it. Instead,

I felt an imbalance between work, family and faith. I was being pulled in opposite directions because I couldn't see that God's plan needed to be intertwined in all three aspects of my life. I took for granted that family and faith would survive without my undivided attention. I had become blinded by all of the nice things that creation could bring, never considering that God was the one who had given me everything I had.

In the Book of Genesis, the Bible shares a story about a man named Abraham. He was a faithful servant to God and knew all that he had were gifts provided by God. By the world's standards, Abraham was powerful and wealthy. He possessed a lot of land, cattle, gold and silver. However, it wasn't until he was over 100 years old that God gave Abraham his greatest gift, his son Isaac.

Abraham was so faithful to God that everything in his life, including his son, came second to his faith. He was even willing to sacrifice his son to God. Yet, we can't sacrifice even an hour of our time to study Scripture each evening.

The world saw Abraham as a man who had everything, but he saw himself as a man who possessed nothing. We choose to hold tightly to all of our possessions, while we loosely hold on to our faith. The truth is we love creation more than we love God. We have more fear over losing what we have obtained than we fear God Himself.

When we place God first in our lives, it becomes clear that all that we have accumulated, including our time on earth, are gifts provided by God. Even our talents are gifts that He has given us. Nothing we have is our own. Therefore, how can we boast about our talents and worldly possessions if everything belongs to God? Every material thing we possess will perish. However, the one thing that will never perish is God's immense love for us. He knows our selfish ways and observes our selfish desires, but despite our ugliness, He loves us so much that He allowed His only Son to suffer and die so that we could live forever. It is His unconditional love that God longs for us to discover as our greatest possession among all that we have.

Our hearts are being pulled in different directions as we struggle to find our place in the midst of the battle for our attention. We want to give more to family and faith, but we battle for time to make this happen. We long to live an abundant life, but without God, our days will be nothing more than the mundane routine of a shallow existence.

Contentment and balance can be achieved only when our desire to please God becomes stronger than our desire to please creation. Success will be achieved when we see things from God's point of view instead of our own personal gain. When we live for creation, we make choices that go against faith. When we live for God, creation becomes an instrument used by God to grow in our faith.

We are fooling ourselves by not recognizing that all we have is from God because, truthfully, we never intended to make God a priority in our life. We choose to let creation run our lives and keep our Creator at a distance. It is easier to live in darkness than illuminate things with the light God provides. We allow creation to define who we are instead of living for the purpose our Creator has for us. The choice to live selfishly over living for our faith is the most destructive weapon we have.

"It seems to be a fact of life that when I want to do what is right, I inevitably do what is wrong. I love God's law with all my heart. But there is another law at work within me that is at war with my mind. This law wins the fight and makes me a slave to the sin that is still within me."

ROMANS 7:21–23

God puts us in situations for His purpose, although many of us only see the advantages or disadvantages from our personal limited perspective. Looking back on my career, I can now see where moments of connecting with God were missed simply because I was too busy and involved in my affairs. Yet, He placed people in my life to show me His way. It's not the job that I remember, or even the title that I held, but it's the people with whom I worked that stand out in my mind. It becomes clear to see God in one's life when we look at our situations from His perspective instead of our own.

When pursuing a new career, or finding happiness in your current job, when was the last time you sought God's advice concerning the matter? A coworker of mine was going through a career change at the age of 45. This is a difficult step for many because most of us hope to have job security by that age, but we soon discover that nothing that comes from creation is secure. I remember having lunch with her and talking about possible career opportunities. She was looking for my advice, and the only advice I had was to suggest that she pray about it.

Her expression appeared quite curious and surprised. I will never forget her response. "Well, when I pray, I know things happen in God's time. But I need a job today, so waiting for His response is not an option."

When we choose to place God first in our lives, we come to realize that our time is actually His time given to us. Perhaps her life was in a holding pattern so that when everything else was exhausted, she would finally come to Him in prayer for direction.

One of the greatest gifts God gave me was down time. I had been working forty-hour weeks, raising a family with my husband, and trying to stay on top of everything. Exhaustion was a constant companion. For the first time in over twenty years, God created down time for me so I could have moment of quietness. Creation was no longer sending me e-mails, demanding my time and attention, and drowning me in the daily schedule of my life.

Admittedly, some days were almost too quiet. It's easy to become anxious when facing times of uncertainty. That is what creation does to our hearts. It reminds us that bills need to be paid and life's activities need to be addressed.

However, this time allowed me to pursue my faith, and I began developing a relationship with God. When we pursue God's advice in moments like these, things will fall into place. The key is praying for advice that fulfills what He wants of us and evaluating our options where serving Him becomes the first item on our list of criteria.

Any profession can be a calling if God's purpose prevails. We make the corporate world a weapon to be used against our Creator when actually it can become a means to serve God's purpose. I wasted many working years unaware that my job could have been used to serve God. Creation teaches us to dedicate endless hours of time and effort to jobs in order to achieve wealth. Many may have called me a workaholic. If being a workaholic meant there wasn't time given to God, then that's exactly what I was. Work was my weapon against my faith, using it as an excuse for not giving more of myself to God.

Rest assured, God wants us to live a wonderful life, and many of His blessings represent our abilities to provide for our needs by using the talents He gave us. The challenge becomes when we lose balance by focusing more on the gifts than on the Giver. We often miss those moments that God calls to us, trying desperately to draw us nearer to Him. He fights endlessly for our attention and uses all that He can to move our hearts toward Him. Sometimes He wins through our pain and suffering. Often God loses through our prosperity and success.

Here is the good news: When everyone else gives up on you, including your job, friends—and even family—God continues battling for our attention, and most importantly, our hearts.

Vacations can be those times when a tiny bit of His call slips through. It is moments like these when we surround ourselves in His beautiful creation that we truly experience relaxation and peace in the world. There is nothing better than spending time in the mountains or on a quiet beach. We dread Monday morning and having to return to reality.

Perhaps it is not reality that we dread, but all that it has become. Where is the peace and serenity in our daily lives? Where are the moments of relaxation? Why must we travel to get away from it all? We live for our creation, yet look forward to getting away from it. Perhaps God has provided us too much. We have come to enjoy all that He has given us and neglect to see Him as the Giver in our lives. We see His blessings as things and events that we've created for ourselves. Taking credit for all that we have is a weapon used against our faith.

"So they worshiped the things God made but not the Creator himself, who is to be praised forever."

ROMANS 1:25

Which side are you on in this battle? How many other weapons do we use for excuses to arm ourselves against giving more of ourselves to God? At what point will we surrender our time and hearts to our faith? Do we even want to surrender? Are we willing to take the risk?

When we place our faith first in our lives, we see for the first time that the choices we make affect not only today, but also our day of judgment. When I left corporate America, I told people I had no choice. I was called to do what God needed me to do. This statement bewildered most, including myself.

I could have stayed at the job and continue to look at the events that had occurred as mere coincidences in my life. However, when we stop living for creation, we learn that there are no coincidences in life. Things really do happen for a reason, and by opening up our hearts, we can begin experiencing God's work firsthand in our lives. Today is more than just a day; it is an opportunity to live life for Him and do His will instead of bowing to the will of others. Presumption is sin, and when we presume that tomorrow will come and we will get to our matters of faith tomorrow, we are only fooling ourselves. We promise starting tomorrow that we will begin living for God and not creation. However, tomorrow does not come for everyone, and our delay can be the most destructive weapon we use against our faith.

When our day of judgment comes, God will not ask how much money we have, but instead how we used it to help those in need. He will not concern Himself with the size of our home, but with how often we opened our doors to our neighbors and friends. He will ignore the type of car we drove, but will take note of how often we transported those who had no means of transportation. God will not be consumed with how much we loved His creation, but with how we used His creation to fulfill His purpose. God will look at what is at the top of our list of priorities.

At some point, we see that the weapons we use are merely excuses in our lives. Our desire to pursue a relationship with God is nonexistent. We will defend ourselves for years—and what may appear to be a winning track record of good deeds will be nothing more than serving selfish desires.

When we honestly look at ourselves in the mirror, we see multiple wounds and the pain that caused them, but we don't have to live with the scars. We will eventually have to surrender, but we don't have to be destroyed.

God's hope is that our choices build endurance and our suffering becomes our strength from the hope we obtain through our faith. When we open our hearts and allow Him in, we experience victory, acknowledging our weapons are useless against Him and life is meaningless without Him.

God's presence never leaves our side. Have you ever driven along a highway, surrounded by cement roads, buildings and billboards, only to catch a quick glimpse of a flower growing in the crack of the road? It is moments like these that remind me that His presence will always prevail. Nothing can hold Him back. When we choose to place our faith at the center of our lives, our weapons are replaced with God's love and devotion. Our desires for success become measured by how well we live up to God's expectations and not our own. It doesn't mean that we stop sinning, but our desires to become like Christ come to the forefront ahead of everything else.

So many of us never achieve this level of faith. We never come to know God and experience His plan that He has prepared for us. We choose to live our lives separate from faith, refusing to see God's purpose. The lives that we have created and the possessions we have obtained have become far more significant than our Creator Himself. Living a compromising and demoralizing lifestyle is strictly forbidden. Those who claim to know God but choose a lifestyle that goes against His principles deny Christ in their lives.

Solomon, in the midst of his greatness, often referred to the meaning of life without God as like chasing the wind. When our focus becomes solely on the things of this world, we lose sight of what God longs for us to become. When we choose to live for God, an amazing transformation takes place. Our hearts, once filled with anxiety, become at ease and light. We learn to trust Him with all of our burdens, accepting that if tomorrow comes, it is gift from God as a means to draw us closer to Him. It's not to say that our problems will go away or that life becomes easier to face. However, what we see as a problem, He will use as an opportunity to build endurance in the battle for our hearts.

Living for God over creation creates endless opportunities and will bring victory in finding meaning and purpose in every aspect of our lives. The world we live in is far worse off today than ever before. I'm not being pessimistic. It's the truth. However, the wars taking take place today in the news are minimal compared to the battle Christ is fighting to win over our hearts.

"God has given gifts to each of you from his great variety of spiritual gifts. Manage them well so that God's generosity can flow through you."

1 PETER 4:10

All of creation will eventually be destroyed, so living for it is worthless. Living for our faith is imperative to receiving life forever. It is the only way, and the only battle that is worth fighting for.

"If your sinful nature controls your mind, there is death. But if the Holy Spirit controls your mind, there is life and peace."

ROMANS 8:6

It becomes our choice to make. Which side do we choose to take: creation or Creator?

Chapter Fourteen

MAKING A DIFFERENCE

*"But even more blessed are all who hear the word of God
and put it into practice."*

LUKE 11:28

I attended a going-away party for a coworker of mine who had been with the company for over seventeen years. Seventeen years is a long time in today's corporate environment. I asked him that evening what he felt were his biggest contributions to the company.

His response was that he had generated well over $20,000,000 in revenue to the bottom line. He had put in thousands of hours of time and dedication to meeting and exceeding corporate goals and expectations.

I then asked if he felt like he had made a difference. At first, I wasn't sure he had understood my question. He thought for quite some time, and then his eyes shifted to the floor. When he finally looked up, he replied, "I don't know."

He had given seventeen years of his life and didn't know if he had made any difference in the company or in the lives of the people who worked with him. Unfortunately, this type of response is very common in the corporate world. For the past twenty years of my career, I honestly can't say whether I made a difference either. However, in business, our success is not measured by the impact we had on people's lives but on our contributions we made to the bottom line. We are here today and gone tomorrow. That is life in the corporate world.

Unfortunately, for many, how we view our personal lives is no different than business. We measure our success by the lifestyle we live. We think the difference we make is based on our level of influence and socioeconomic status. Money and power are the tools we use to gauge how much of a difference we make. So if we don't have a lot of money or power, then how can we truly make a difference in the world today?

The most significant differences we can make in this life cannot be bought with money or earned through power and authority. It is a virtue that is instilled in every human being—young and old, rich and poor alike. Making a difference has to do with the actions we take and measuring our success by the standards found in Scripture, instead of by the standards provided by this world.

In the story of Micah found in the Bible, God reveals His three expectations that use His standards for how we can truly make a difference in our lives and those around us:

1. Do what is right;
2. Love kindness;
3. Walk humbly with our Lord.

If you were to leave your job today, could you say you had made a difference by living up to these three standards? We may have had moments of fulfilling these criteria, but how loyal are we to live by God's standards in every aspect of our working and personal lives?

God hasn't made it complicated. We're the ones who have complicated it because in general, these three criteria go against what the world expects of us if we're trying to make a difference. In the corporate world, doing what is right may depend on who benefits the most. Kindness creates barriers to our system of beliefs because power and authority are not always kind in principle. Walking humbly with our Lord may require us to walk against our company. It is these three expectations that create the battle over where our loyalty lies.

DO WHAT IS RIGHT

I was exposed to a compromising situation in the corporate world that may have resulted in my termination had I brought the matter to the attention of certain people. I once witnessed one of our executives use corporate revenue to cover some of his personal living expenses. Although the company didn't know it, they were paying the rent for the very nice condominium where he lived. This was nearly a $30,000 annual expenditure. I was asked to make sure the contract was signed by the client and forwarded to my boss for approval.

Perhaps the company thought I wouldn't figure out what was going on. Or perhaps they justified it as such a small expense it would quietly slip through the cracks. Although I was very disturbed by this matter, I decided to look the other way and never speak a word about what was happening. Sad to say, everyone else looked the other way as well, including the company president and the accounting department. We all sacrificed our integrity and doing what was right because our fear of losing our jobs was greater than our fear of God's judgment for our actions.

When we allow practices like this to happen in our business world, we go against doing what is right in God's eyes. We would rather risk losing our integrity than conduct ourselves according to the standards provided by our faith. It's sad but true. Making a difference will require us to stand up for what is right, even if it means being abandoned by those around us. We know things are black and white, but we settle for gray, poorly justifying the reason for our actions. My justification was that I needed to keep my job. But is any job really worth keeping if you have to sacrifice your dignity for it? Making a difference is doing what is right no matter what the consequences may be. Anything less is denying God in our lives.

The story of Daniel is one of the best examples of an individual who would rather stand alone and do what is right than sacrifice his integrity. The Book of Daniel is about a young hand-picked leader who was willing to give up his life for God. He feared God above everything else in this world. Ironically it was this fear that provided him the security and safety in his life.

In Babylon, where Daniel lived after being taken there as a captive when the king of Babylon defeated Israel, the king ordered the people to pray to no other gods except the king himself. Daniel absolutely refused the king's command and continued to pray openly to God. He was thrown into a den of lions for standing up for what he believed.

We are thrown into a lions' den every day by being exposed to compromising situations. We turn the other way to avoid any repercussion, but the repercussion is the guilt that remains deep within us. What's even worse is when others throw us into the den to hide their involvement.

In the corporate world, we refer to this as the "fall guy." Someone must take the blame to protect the guilty. However, in the end, everyone will face destruction. Many will refuse to do what is right because we feel that what's right according to God's standard may be too much to ask of ourselves. Can we afford to risk our jobs over trusting our faith?

When we live our life with this mentality, we are thinking short-term. We live only for today because we limit our successes to what we are able to obtain in this world. We give no consideration to what this will mean in obtaining eternal life. We live without fear of God when we think only about living for today and not living for the possibility of eternal life. Isn't God's grace so great that He will forgive us?

> "So since God's grace has set us free from the law, does this mean we can go on sinning? Of course not! Don't you realize that whatever you choose to obey becomes your master? You can choose sin, which leads to death, or you can choose to obey God and receive his approval."

ROMANS 6:15–16

The answer is yes, but only through repentance and believing in Christ. Time does not make our sins go away. We may forget about them over time, or justify how insignificant they really were. We were young and naïve, or old and senile. Whatever our excuse is to forget, God's memory is perfect and nothing slips by. We are not forgiven simply by placing matters in the back of our minds. Repenting is our only means of erasing the scars.

Because we can't achieve perfection, which is Christ, should we even try?

The answer is yes again. We can come up with hundreds of excuses why we can't fulfill God's purpose for us. For many, it becomes too uncomfortable. We suddenly find ourselves outside the norm when we follow the standards of our faith. It's more attractive to be part of the popular group than associate ourselves with losers or nerds.

For others, it becomes too great of a risk. I wasn't willing to risk my job over trusting that God would take care of me. We don't like to rock the boat, so turning our backs becomes less risky than turning toward our faith. We convince ourselves that it really isn't that big a deal.

In God's eyes, it is a big deal. Every day He gives us matters greatly to Him, and He gives us many opportunities to choose to live by the standards of our faith. God reaches for us every day, but we are reaching the other way. He hopes the people He places in our lives will bring us closer to Him. Yet, we don't see into other's hearts to hear what they're really telling us. We miss God's calling by denying that He even called out to us. We fail to see that the things currently going wrong in our lives may be His way of getting our attention.

It became more and more difficult for me to tolerate questionable business tactics in the corporate world. God had to make it ugly—and even personal—before I humbly heard His voice and finally agreed to obey. We must stop making excuses because eventually excuses fall on deaf ears. We must stop living for ourselves because living for our own desires means not desiring to grow in our faith. We will never be perfect, but we must never stop trying to live as perfectly as Christ showed us how to live. It will be difficult and often uncomfortable, but God's standards outweigh any risk that we may face in our lives.

Making a difference will mean doing what is right and accepting the fact that many will abandon us because we choose to live for Him and not ourselves. We will face persecution and many will enjoy watching us fall. However, our actions are not about honoring ourselves, but about honoring Him who asks us to live as His example.

"You can enter God's Kingdom only through the narrow gate. The highway to hell is broad, and its gate is wide for the many who choose the easy way. But the gateway to life is small, and the road is narrow, and only a few ever find it."

Matthew 7:13–14

Love kindness

The word "kind" is rarely spoken about it any type of training or management course provided in the corporate world. In fact, the word "kindness" goes against the grain of how we perceive corporate leadership today. What is it about the word "kind" that makes it a "four-letter word" in the corporate environment?

The perception is that to be effective in the corporate world, you have to be hard on the outside. In fact, as a woman in management, I found this to be even more critical if I wanted to be taken seriously. Women managers are often perceived as being more emotional and softhearted because we are female. I was once the only female manager for a company I worked with. I often found myself having to exaggerate my hardness in my management style so my male counterparts would not perceive me as being "weak." Women often feel that we have to be tough to get beyond the stigma of being softer just because we're female.

What would happen if a company decided to place kindness at the top of the list of qualities to model? Do we really believe being hard and abrasive brings in more revenue than being kind? Is it really a means of motivating? Or is it manipulating?

Random acts of kindness in a corporate environment can be the difference in what makes a job fulfilling versus what makes a job destructive. Here are just a few examples of random acts of kindness to consider:

1. Acknowledge others for their accomplishments, despite how big or small.
2. Conduct meetings where every voice is heard with respect and appreciation.

3. Provide support to an employee experiencing a personal problem or tragedy.
4. Work together as a team, even when performance is not at its peak.
5. Shut down all gossip in the office.
6. Greet the receptionist as though this person is the most important individual in the company.
7. Never lose your temper—no matter what.
8. Never put down others.
9. Use words of strength and encouragement.
10. Allow for mistakes and show your team how they can grow from them.
11. Prohibit wrongdoing in a company. Always do what is right.
12. Allow a parent to leave early for family obligations.
13. Have coffee with individuals several levels below you, including the person who delivers your mail each day.
14. Take time to reflect on why several of your best employees have resigned; admit your actions need to change.
15. Measure individuals not on efficiency, but on character.
16. Value someone else's time more than your own.
17. Never ask someone to do something that you wouldn't do yourself.
18. Lead through serving others first.
19. Don't be afraid to set an example, even if it means failing in front of your peers.
20. Cultivate the ability to listen with your heart, beyond the words of an e-mail.
21. Be kind and courteous at all times.

In the corporate world, kindness is associated with weakness. One of the biggest misconceptions in business today is that individuals who are kind are considered weak and unable to be effective leaders.

In a previous chapter, I talked about Joseph as one of the most influential and powerful leaders of biblical times. However, one of his greatest attributes as a leader was his ability to be kind. Joseph was second in charge over the country of Egypt, just under Pharaoh. In the corporate world, he would have had the title of President.

Famine had taken over the land and Joseph's primary responsibility was distributing the food among the people and collecting money from them for it. When his brothers came from their faraway country for food, Joseph could have refused to give them any and allowed them to starve to death. These were the same brothers who had plotted to take Joseph's life. What reason would he have to spare their lives? There is only one explanation for Joseph's kindness: He was living by the standards of his faith.

Joseph never looked at the events in his life with bitterness or resentment. He knew his brothers meant evil, but in Joseph's heart, he knew that God meant it for good. He had every reason to turn his back on faith and go against those who had wronged him. The world would have told him his actions were justified and that any act of kindness would have been a sign of weakness by its standards.

Joseph's kindness was not a reflection of weakness, but of his compassion for his family and his faith. Judging others is this world is meaningless when we consider the judgment we face from God when we take revenge against those who have hurt us either physically or emotionally.

It is easy to allow cynicism to enter our hearts because of the events of our lives, justifying our sentiments by the world's standards. We blame our bosses for our performance. We blame our spouses or parents for the wrongs in our lives. We blame our children for our inadequacies, and then we blame God when life falls apart.

There was no blame in Joseph's heart. There was not the slightest bit of cynicism or anger toward anyone who had wronged him. Every moment of his life, whether it was joy or tribulation, success or suffering, Joseph remained strong in his faith and kind to all—whether they had helped him or hurt him. Joseph did what was right and acted with kindness and compassion.

Genuine leaders are not abrasive or harsh in their style of management. They don't live their lives with cynicism and bitterness. In fact, one of their greatest attributes is their kindness and the respect they have for their teams. This kindness pours into their families. There is nothing more gratifying to see than a husband and wife care for each other after fifty years of being together.

There is nothing more heartfelt than seeing a child share a favorite toy with a friend. There is nothing more admired than seeing kindness as the response of someone who has been wronged, falsely accused, or was the subject of today's gossip. These are examples of how we are called to live our lives.

We are called to provide random acts of kindness. When we use our hearts, it becomes a natural thing to do. Kindness occurs when we look to our faith in handling matters of conflict. I have found that when I involve God in matters of conflict, being angry or resentful is never an option. Anger rarely solves conflict. In fact, it is like gasoline that is ready to burst into flames when poured on a fire. Only faith will dissolve whatever issues are stirring anger and cynicism in our heart.

Kindness keeps one levelheaded and can truly be an admirable quality when used in moments of conflict. Have you ever remained calm around someone who is trying so desperately to pick a fight? Kindness is an admirable quality to exemplify, especially around individuals who are abrasive and arrogant. Kindness can only come from the heart, which is where our true character is exposed.

God shows us how to use our hearts in handling matters big and small. He is the one who softens a hard heart and washes the bitterness away. It is impossible to hold a grudge when you have God actively involved in your life. His involvement is what changes an abrasive heart to a kind and compassionate one.

No one is too important to be kind. We consider it acceptable behavior for individuals to walk all over each other and wonder how they achieved their position in the first place. We don't need any more managers. What we need are individuals with a servant mindset who are kind and take the time to let their people know how important their contributions are to the company. Words of appreciation and acts of kindness will create a level of loyalty among your employees, giving you 110 percent of their efforts.

WALK HUMBLY WITH OUR LORD

When I made the decision to study Scripture, I have to admit my intentions were not at first about building my relationship with God. I knew there would be a time when my children would ask if I had ever read the Bible, and I wanted to honestly answer yes to that question. My motivation wasn't about becoming a better person. I was motivated simply by believing it was the right thing to do, never realizing the impact it would have on my life.

I started reading the Bible by being part of a Bible study at our church. It required almost an hour's worth of reading every night, but by the end of the course, we would cover nearly 80 percent of Scripture. Each night, we were assigned certain passages to read and then to answer questions in our workbook. Although these questions didn't appear to have anything to do with my life, the more I read, the more the words spoke directly to the actions of my life.

Reading the Bible is one of life's most rewarding experiences, and yet it is excruciating at the same time. Scripture boldly points out our flaws and areas of weakness. It provides a true reflection of who we really are and how we are supposed to appear to the world. The deeper I read, the more I found myself apologizing to God for my actions, understanding for the first time what repentance really meant.

All this time, I thought I had so much to bring to God, only to learn that there was nothing I could bring. I was only to receive. It was truly the most humbling moment of my life.

I had clearly placed everything above Him. I had valued my socio-economic status more than I had valued a relationship with Him. I had become more concerned about the contents of my home than the content of my heart. It was a painful experience for me to see my actions through God's eyes and identify what I had become. I was so caught up with the events of the world that I had left my faith behind. Reading the newspaper had taken precedence over reading the Bible. Watching TV came before giving thanks to Him. I had placed everything in this world before my faith—until the day I began studying Scripture. It was absolutely a life-changing event.

"For the word of God is full of living power. It is sharper that the sharpest knife, cutting deep into our innermost thoughts and desires. It exposes us

for what we really are. Nothing in all creation can hide from him. Every-thing is naked and exposed before his eyes. This is the God to whom we must explain all that we have done."

HEBREWS 4:12–13

We spend countless hours in the business world taking training courses, listening to motivational speakers and reading articles on how to be successful. We come home and perch in front of our TV's and computer, filling our minds with additional noise and interruptions. Information derived from human origin has become more important than information derived from divine origin.

If you never read the Bible, rest assured you will never be the best you can be. What we consider to be an accomplishment may be viewed as our greatest weakness in God's eyes. Wisdom cannot be found in the news or any business textbook. Wisdom comes by learning through Scripture, studying it and applying it to every part of your life. The Bible teaches us how to walk humbly with God and understand how He plays a role in every aspect of our lives. His Word clearly illustrates how we are nothing without Him and how seeking His advice is what provides us authenticity and core values.

Our lives here on earth are a fleeting moment, and spending all of our time pleasing others instead of pleasing God will never lead us to a fulfilling and prosperous life. If you really want to make a difference, stop spending all of your time concerned about the events of the world and focus on what God wants from you.

Attending a church service once a week is not enough. One must read and study God's Word to truly understand what a relationship with Him is meant to be and the difference it can make. Reading the Bible exposes all of our sins and allows us to humbly acknowledge His continuous love and grace. Reading Scripture will not only impact our lives, it will also show us how to make a difference in other lives by living as an example of our faith.

chapter Fifteen

A RISK
WORTH TAKING

"God blesses you who are hungry now, for you will be satisfied.
God blesses you who weep now, for
the time will come when you will laugh with joy.
God blesses you who are hated and excluded and mocked and cursed
because you are identified with me, the Son of Man."

LUKE 6:21–22

Beginning my life in corporate America was a very exciting time. I remember my first job and receiving my first paycheck. It is a very rewarding experience to be able to support myself and live the American dream. Climbing the corporate ladder can create opportunities for success and prosperity. For many, however, it becomes a risk as the demands of the job overtake our time for anything else. God desires us to be successful. He wants us to live a harmonious life and have all of our needs met. The question that each of us face is who are we willing to risk more for—God or man?

In the Book of Genesis, we learn about Noah and how he built the ark that saved both his family and God's creation of animals. Noah must have had embarrassing moments when others ridiculed him for building a boat to save him from the flood God said He was going to bring. Nothing like that had ever happened before, yet Noah was willing to take the risk of believing God instead of believing the world. Noah wasn't concerned about what others thought of him, but only about what God's purpose was in his life. Noah truly acted on faith, despite what others must have said about his actions. No one could see the flood coming, but Noah's actions were not based on man's opinion, but on complete and total faith in God.

I didn't have the guts that Noah had when I resigned. I couldn't physically come out and say that I was leaving so I could write a book on Christian principles for corporate America. Admittedly, I was more concerned about what people would think than what God thought of me. Despite my cowardly actions, God gave me the courage to leave anyway. God had a different plan for me.

After time passed, I was able to tell people what made me decide to write a book. The reactions were very interesting. Some people gravitated to me, while others ran far away. I even prayed that God would change His plan for me and have someone else write the book. But His words spoke softly inside my heart, encouraging me that this was what He wanted me to do, reminding me I could trust Him that everything would be OK.

It is this trust that we see as a huge risk in our lives. I found myself trusting the instability of the stock market more than I trusted the words written in the Bible. If I couldn't physically see it, how could I trust it? The problem we face is that we don't look deep enough. When we limit our vision to what's in front of us, we limit our potential regarding what awaits us.

"It was by faith that Noah built an ark to save his family from the flood. He obeyed God, who warned him about something that had never happened before. By his faith he condemned the rest of the world and was made right in God's sight."

HEBREWS 11:7

Noah wasn't given a vision of a flood. What he was given was a heart that opened itself to hearing God's words over the noise in his life. He listened, and more importantly he obeyed, knowing that following the advice of the world actually involves a much greater risk than following the advice of God.

Each day we are given is a special gift, and it is God's hope that we seize every moment in time as an opportunity to grow in our faith. The questions become: What price are you willing to pay? What risks are you willing to take?

When I finally confessed what prompted my writing this book, many of my former associates warned that publishing it would leave me blackballed from ever getting a job again in corporate America. Many people exited my life, and at times, I wondered if I had made the right decision. It is a risk when we look at our lives through God's eyes because all that we have thought to be important becomes obsolete.

How can someone really live a life where faith is intertwined in every aspect, including work and home? It is very hard to do at times, but it can be done when you see the risk as being the greatest reward. The day I resigned, I remember driving out of the parking lot and saying to myself, OK, God, I now work for You.

Are we ready to take the risk? I'm not saying that we should all leave our jobs to follow our faith. The message that I personally gained was to follow my faith and it would lead me to the next job. It is hard to relinquish our control to something we believe in when our fear of the unknown is greater than our beliefs. Because we can't see into our future, uncertainty enters our hearts and causes us to begin questioning our actions. This questioning can potentially lead to our destruction if we let it get the upper hand in our thinking.

John the Baptist spoke reverently about taking the risk and changing our wayward lives. John had no power or authority within the Jewish political system, yet his words changed the hearts of many of those who listened. John preached in the middle of the wilderness, perhaps to get away from the noise and distractions of life. His words were forceful, and he didn't hold anything back as he exposed our sinful deeds and motives. However, his strong choice of words was a reflection of his conviction behind his faith. John powerfully challenged people who claimed to be God-followers to prove it by the way they lived their lives. He was willing to take the risk for his faith over everything else in his life. Here is a sample of John's preaching:

"You brood of snakes! Who warned you to flee God's coming judgment? Prove by the way you live that you have really turned from your sins and turned to God. Don't just say, 'We're safe-we're descendants of Abraham.' That proves nothing. God can change these stones here into children of Abraham. Even now the ax of God's judgment is poised, ready to sever your roots. Yes, every tree that does not produce good fruit will be chopped down and thrown in the fire."

LUKE 3:7-9

Our fear of publicly proclaiming our faith, especially in the business world, is greater than our fear of God. This is not about standing on a street corner and reciting Bible verses for the crowds. God isn't asking us to be a fanatic. However, it is about giving God credit for everything in our lives and recognizing His purpose and divine control.

We claim to be Christians, but when we leave our churches, we deny Him in our actions. We are provided His Word, but we never make time to read it or apply it to our lives. We don't worry about Judgment Day because our minds tell us that day is so far in the future. As a result, we live for today, focusing on providing for our own selfish needs instead of pursuing what God wants us to.

God is patiently waiting, but at what point will His patience run out?

Are we so blind to our actions that we cannot see our greed? Have we become so arrogant, thinking we don't need to read the Bible because we already know all we need in order to get along in this world? Have our hearts become so hard that all we feel is numbness to any possibility of His existence?

"Then Jesus prayed this prayer: 'O Father, Lord of heaven and earth, thank you for hiding the truth from those who think themselves so wise and clever, and for revealing it to the childlike. Yes Father, it pleased you to do it this way!'"

MATTHEW 11:25–26

We are fooling ourselves by believing we are living right in God's eyes when we won't take the risk of living for Him. If we continue to live by the world's standards, then we have determined that our importance is defined by sin and not faith.

When we stop to think about it, what are we risking when we place God above everything else? What is lost from this risk, and more importantly, what is gained?

For me personally, I did lose a sense of belonging. Many people who I considered friends, quietly slipped away. I don't know if a business would hire me today now that I have been so public about my beliefs. However, I do believe there are people and companies who will open their doors to us because of our commitment to our faith.

Most importantly, here is what I have personally gained: purpose and meaning to my life. I know exactly where I am, and I have a steady plan on where I'm going. Although I can't see down the road, I know I am going in the right direction.

This is not to say I won't make mistakes along the way. However, when you no longer live to please the world, you have no fear of admitting you've made a mistake because God will show you how to correct it. You have no fear of apologizing for your mistakes because your fear of God and what He thinks becomes greater than our insecurities of what the world may think of us.

Here is the good news: God erases all of our past simply by asking for forgiveness with a humble heart. God will help prepare us for anything that we face simply because He loves us so much. God will place people in our lives at times when we feel we don't belong, simply because He wants us to remain encouraged and faithful. God will provide for our every need, simply because we've placed our trust into Him. When we stop to think about it, is it really that great of a risk?

Jobs will come and go. People will remain by our sides, or quietly slip away. Success will knock at our door, while tragedy is lurking in our hallways. When our faith is placed first, we are able to survive both the good and bad times. The risk of following our faith becomes the soundest investment we can ever make. God doesn't make mistakes; therefore, when things happen, we can feel confident that it is all for our better because He is in control. It provides a 100 percent return on our investment of time. Taking the risk for our faith only means living the life He so desperately desires for each of us.

> "Do not throw away this confident trust in the Lord, no matter what happens. Remember the great reward it brings you! Patient endurance is what you need now, so you will continue to do God's will. They you will receive all that he has promised"

HEBREWS 10:35–36

chapter sixteen

WILL YOU BE LEFT BEHIND?

*"If the righteous are barely saved, what chance
will the godless and sinners have?"*

1 PETER 4:18

One morning I was having coffee with a dear friend who showed me the cover story of one of the local newspapers that claimed our city is one of the safest communities in the nation.

Compared to other cities, crime is very low in our community. We are blessed to have a wonderful environment to raise our families. On the outside of our homes, everything appears to be safe and secure. The beautiful landscaped yards and quiet settings create the illusion that everything is perfect and happy.

Often the lives we lead reflect the same sense of false security. Our jobs pay the bills and provide 401(k)s for our future savings. We bank on the promise from our companies that we will be valued for our contributions for as long as we remain employed. It is easy to get caught up in this false sense of security, believing that nothing bad is ever going to happen.

What does our future hold? Will the world provide a shield of armor from possible destruction? King David probably thought this when he began to live his life as though he was above God's law, committing adultery and murder during the height of his influence and power. His son Solomon followed a similar path as that of his father. He was also at the highest point of his authority when things began to fall apart.

The world can create a level of deception simply by the words printed in a news headline. We have become so consumed with what we believe our worldly future holds. The question we should be asking is: "Have we put a second thought into God's plan for what our tomorrow holds?"

Here is news that many of us don't want to think about: Some day, every one of us will die. All of our worldly possessions will be left behind. Our beautiful homes, expensive cars and luxurious lifestyles will all perish. Even our important title will be forgotten. As time passes, those who knew us will no longer mention our names. The world will eventually forget who we are and all that we had.

"If anyone acknowledges me publicly here on earth, I will openly acknowledge that person before my Father in heaven. But if anyone denies me here on earth, I will deny that person before my Father in heaven."

MATTHEW 10:32–33

We don't like to believe that we will be forgotten, but it is our reality. I remember when one of our sales executives resigned, deciding it was time to retire and enter a new phase in his life. He had generated millions of dollars for the company and had dedicated endless hours to his clients' success. One Friday afternoon, our company had a going-away party for him, acknowledging all of the contributions he had made to the bottom line.

On Monday morning, I passed by his desk and noticed it had already been filled. A new person was sitting there, unaware of the gentleman who had spent years in that space. As I looked around, it was business as usual. Nothing had stopped, or even changed, other than that a new person had been added to our team. Our former associate had already been forgotten.

Business continues. Life continues. Yet, for some reason, I felt I was left behind. My coworker had moved on to a new phase of life. Something in him had said it was time to leave and pursue a new opportunity. He was only in his late 50s and staying in this environment made him feel like he was being held back.

I was amazed by his courage. He had two kids and a wife. How does one leave this secure working world and face the unknown when bills still must be paid? I remember asking him if he was concerned about his future and was amazed by his response, "When you have faith, your future is the last thing you need to worry about."

My associate was able to see beyond the future the world had to offer. The world's future is limited to an unknown number of days in which your success is determined primarily by the amount of money you have invested for financial security.

The significance of planning financially for our future is critical. Saving is imperative in order to prepare for any unforeseen expenses and to provide the basic necessities. But when we plan only for our worldly lives and not our eternal lives, our days become nothing more than living a routine. Often we feel we are missing something. Shouldn't life have more to offer than waking up, fulfilling our daily responsibilities and going to bed at night?

It's hard to think about things we can't see—and to some extent comprehend. In today's world, our beliefs and standards are formed by what we hear from people we feel are highly influential. If their names are in the news media, we want to read about them.

But when we live only for the standards of this world, we miss God's purpose in our lives, and potentially regret having not done more than what we did.

What does it feel like to be left behind? Have you ever been overlooked for a promotion that went to someone with less experience? Have you ever felt excluded from a social event? Do you spend endless hours trying to keep up with your neighbors and worry they may not be your friend if your lifestyle doesn't mirror a particular socioeconomic level?

Have you ever walked into a party and felt like a stranger to the people you have seen—but not known—for over ten years? I remember feeling like

I was the only working mother in my neighborhood. I had few social contacts because my days were spent in an office, and my evenings were spent at home. It seemed important at that time to be invited to all of the cocktail parties and social engagements, even though we didn't really know anyone. For years, I felt left behind.

When you live only for this world, you not only feel left behind, you *become* left behind. The world's standards change in the blink of an eye. What is the trend today will be old news tomorrow. Yet, we do everything to prevent becoming yesterday's news. Keeping up with the latest fashions and lifestyles of the rich and famous has become the essence of our own existence. We strive to look younger because for some reason, looking our age will make us feel like we're left behind.

There is One who will never forget us or encourage us to be anything different than what He hopes for us to become. He knew us before we were born, was present at every occasion in our lives, and shared laughter and tears behind every success or struggle that we faced. He knows our past. He knows our present. Most importantly, He knows our future.

He allows us to lead our lives any way we want, but He never stops trying to help us find our way. He loves us so much that more than anything, He doesn't want us to be left behind. The world and everything it has to offer will eventually leave you. However, when we pray for His presence in our lives, He remains at our sides. Jesus Christ is the only constant factor in our ever-changing world.

When we can see ourselves through His eyes, and not the eyes of the world, we find being left behind by the world is not a bad thing. In fact, it takes a lot of pressure off us when we don't try to maintain its standards. Living our lives by loving the things of the world means living our lives without love for our faith.

For more years than I want to admit, I lived to please this world. However, the more I tried to please, the further I was left behind. The more I tried to manage my life on my own, the more uncertain I became. God has a way of taking us out of our comfort zones to show us how wonderful it feels to be left behind by the world and enter His.

What the world defines as success, God may see as greed. What the world defines as acceptable, God may find repulsive. What deeds we claim to be good may be acts of selfishness in His eyes. We think we are at the top of our game, but God may see us differently. If you know how the world sees you but remain uncertain about how God sees you, perhaps it's time to view your actions through His eyes. It may not be clearly visible, but the uncertainty that stirs our hearts may be God's way of pushing us to explore further.

Over forty years of my life passed before I even acknowledged that the uncertainty of my life was coming from Him. I always felt happy, but never truly content. Everything was going so well that I didn't feel the urge to explore deeper into my faith. I was living my life inside a bubble where everything appeared so perfect. Yet it was this perfection that brought about my uncertainty. Perhaps I was living in denial that anything I was doing was all that bad in God's eyes. Yet, the fact that I placed more trust in the matters of the world than in Him is one of the greatest sins I or anyone can commit. Placing our matters before our faith means leaving God behind.

Imagine if you knew the moment of your death. How would you choose to live your final days? In the story discussed earlier in this book about Joseph spending several years in prison, he met Pharaoh's cupbearer and chief baker who were also serving jail time. Both of these gentlemen had dreams that Joseph was able to interpret. The meaning behind the dream of the chief baker told of his death and that it would take place in three days. The Bible doesn't share whether or not he discussed his faith with Joseph, but in seventy-two hours, he was dead. Did he even wonder if he would be left behind?

God gives us a lifetime to find the path that leads to Him. Some of us are given many years and others much less. The real tragedy is not the number of years we live or don't live on earth, but the number of years that we live for this world—and not for Him.

The chief baker was lucky. He was told he had three days to change his ways.

We don't know our moment of death, and many of us never consider whether we will be left behind. If we have left God out of our daily affairs, we will be left behind. Salvation is our greatest gift, but because we can't see it, we don't understand the value that it brings.

"I once thought all these things were so very important, but now I consider them worthless because of what Christ has done. Yes, everything else is worthless when compared with the priceless gain of knowing Christ Jesus my Lord."

PHILIPPIANS 3:7–8

The apostle Paul lived many years trying to please the world. He flaunted his knowledge of the Jewish laws and used his position of authority to judge others. He was a powerful leader by the world's standards, and in his eyes, his eternal destiny was secured. However, Paul quickly learned he was living a life of fallacy. Christ revealed to him how misguided his life had become and this led to Paul's transformation. Paul was given a new purpose that was not his own, but God's.

Did life suddenly become easy for Paul? Certainly not. Paul suffered greatly for Christ. He was beaten severely, thrown into prison, and went without food or water over periods of time. Paul even lived with what he referred to as "a thorn in his side." The Bible never defines exactly if this thorn was a physical or emotional ailment. Whatever it was, Paul considered it a weakness that would hinder his ministry. When we see things only from the world's perspective, and not God's, our thorns are often the things that make us feel we're being left behind. Paul even begged God to remove it, but God reminded him that it was his weakness where God could do His best work.

For many, placing our faith before our affairs becomes too great a risk. We say we trust God and our desire is not to be left behind, but are we really prepared to make the sacrifices in order to please Him?

"Since I know it is all for Christ's good, I am quite content with my weaknesses and with insults, hardships, persecutions and calamities. For when I am weak, then I am strong."

2 CORINTHIANS 12:10

When we choose to no longer live for the world, we no longer worry about the things that make us feel like we're being left behind. Our journey becomes one of uncovering God's meaning and purpose and looking at every obstacle as an opportunity to grow stronger in our faith. At some point, we must make a choice to either believe or deny His existence in our lives. The standards that we follow in how we conduct our lives today should be those based on God's Word—not the standards printed in today's tabloid magazines. When His purpose becomes our purpose, we begin to see our weaknesses as the vehicle God will use to reveal His strength.

Being left behind happens to those who never explore the depth of their faith. Many refuse to know God's purpose simply because they have never asked Him to reveal it to them. We think we know the truth, yet we've never read the Bible. We cannot claim ignorance for not knowing God because His presence is revealed in all of His creation.

Placing God first before the world will provide a sense of belonging, and more importantly, the purpose behind existing. It will not be titles or worldly possessions that will give us the security behind the meaning for our lives. It is honoring Him over everything else and recognizing that each day should be lived with a grateful heart for all that He has provided, and most importantly for the life that awaits us upon our departure from this world.

> "But you must not forget, dear friends, that a day is like a thousand years to the Lord, and a thousand years is like a day. The Lord isn't really being slow about his promise to return, as some people think. No, he is being patient for your sake. He does not want anyone to perish, so he is giving more time for everyone to repent. But the day of the Lord will come unexpectedly as a thief. Then the heavens will pass away with a terrible noise, and everything in them will disappear in fire, and the earth and everything on it will be exposed to judgment."

2 PETER 3:8–10

Judgment Day is real. Judgment Day is coming. Judgment awaits each of us. Our goal today should be living for our faith, for fear of being left behind.

It is God's promise that through Christ, no one will be left behind. However, His hope is, by asking the question, "What have you done for Me lately?" our hearts will be moved. Most importantly, God desires us not only to ponder this question, but act upon it. For many, it may be the most important question one ever faces in life.